100 MINI
CROSS STITCH
DESIGNS

ROSEMARY DRYSDALE

First published 2022 by
Guild of Master Craftsman Publications Ltd Castle Place,
166 High Street, Lewes,
East Sussex, BN7 1XU

Reprinted 2023

ISBN 978 1 78494 627 2

A catalogue record for this book is available from
the British Library.

Managing Art Editor: Darren Brant
Art Editor: Jennifer Stephens
Editor: Susan Elliott
Technical Editor: Trisha Malcolm
Photographer: Quail Studio
Stylist: Mose& Styling

Colour origination by GMC Reprographics
Printed and bound in China

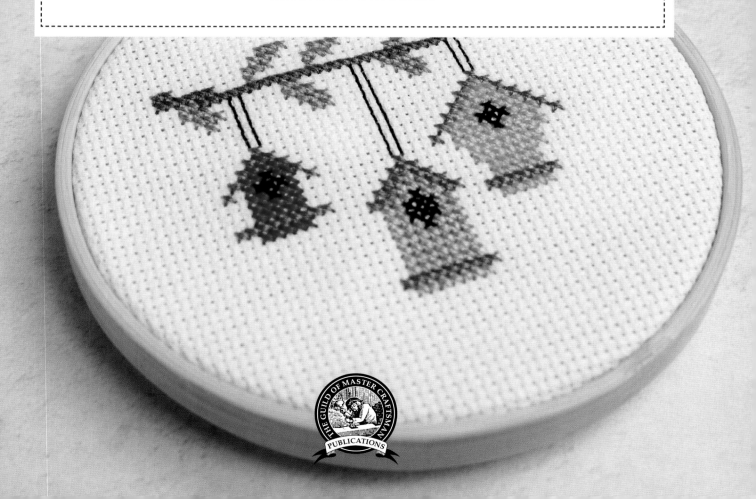

100 MINI
CROSS STITCH
DESIGNS

ROSEMARY DRYSDALE

THE GUILD OF MASTER CRAFTSMAN PUBLICATIONS

CONTENTS

INTRODUCTION

Cross stitching is a relaxing craft consisting of one simple embroidery stitch in the form of an X. This stitch dates back hundreds of years and is found in many cultures, both on clothing and on decorative items, such as samplers.

Cross stitch has become one of the most popular crafts today. Learning to cross stitch is very easy, and the following pages provide all you need to know to master this wonderful technique. Each of the 100 designs are relatively small, so they can be finished in an evening or two.

I have been an embroiderer most of my life and have written many books on every embroidery subject, from blackwork to cross stitch. Working on these little cross-stitched designs has been incredibly relaxing and enjoyable, and I hope

that if you are a new cross stitcher or a lifelong embroiderer, you'll love the process of making these mini designs for yourself or to make something special to give as a gift to friends.

All the designs in this book can be displayed in hoops, as we have done with many of them, and hung on a wall. Alternatively, they can be made into pillows, framed pictures, cards, pincushions and sachets. You can also use them to adorn clothing, linens and items for the home. There are endless possibilities!

I hope you grow to love cross stitch as much as I do.

Rosemary

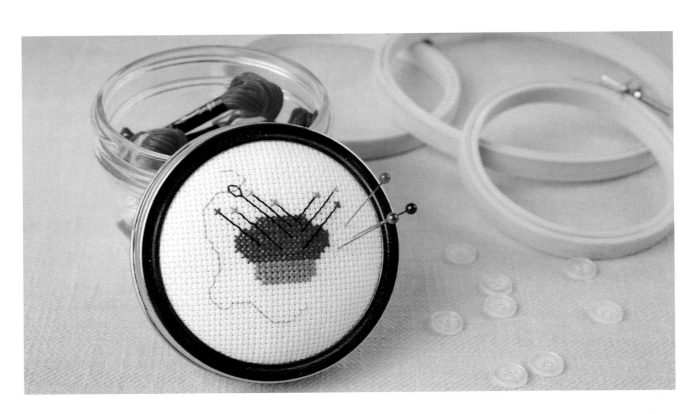

TOOLS AND MATERIALS

Before starting to cross stitch, you'll need to gather some essential items. If you are a sewer, you probably already have some of the basic tools on hand. The fabrics, threads and embroidery hoops you'll need are readily available at craft and fabric shops, and they are generally quite affordable.

NEEDLES

Always use a good-quality tapestry needle with an eye large enough to allow the thread to slide easily through it. Blunt-pointed needles are used to work on cross stitch fabrics because they slide easily between the fabric threads, and through the holes between the threads, without piercing or splitting the fabric. They are sold as tapestry or cross stitch needles, have a large eye, and come in a variety of sizes—the higher the number, the finer the needle. I used a size 24 needle for all the designs in this book. A size 26 needle would also work, but it is a smaller needle and a little more difficult to thread. If you are having trouble threading, you might want to use a needle threader.

Do not leave the needle in the work when you are not stitching, as it can leave a mark.

If you are mounting your stitching in a hoop, you will need a tapestry needle for gathering the backs, and a large-eyed, pointed embroidery needle to sew the felt backing in place.

SCISSORS

It's essential to have high-quality scissors to ensure clean cuts every time. You will need:
- A sharp, pointed pair of small embroidery scissors with narrow blades for cutting threads.
- A large pair of sharp fabric scissors for cutting fabrics only.

FABRICS

Cross stitch is also called counted cross stitch because the design is not stamped on the fabric. Instead, it is worked by counting the stitches from a chart onto an even-weave fabric according to the fabric threads.

Most of the designs in this book (all of those in hoops) are worked on Aida cloth. This fabric, used primarily for cross stitch, has threads woven into a series of small squares divided by tiny holes. It is measured by how many squares are woven into 1in (2.5cm); a 14-count Aida has 14 squares woven into 1in (2.5cm). Some designs (some framed projects, for example) were worked on an 11-count Aida, with 11 squares woven per inch, creating a larger design.

Linen is another fabric of choice for counted cross stitch designs and gives a finer look. Linen is a little more challenging to work with than Aida cloth, as the threads are finer and designs have to be worked over two fabric threads. So, to get 14 stitches per inch, you need a 28-count linen and you work each stitch over two threads, giving you 14 stitches per inch.

Always choose the best quality fabric in a natural fibre for your stitching. Both Aida and linen are available in a variety of colours and counts, and you can experiment with them to create interesting effects. To be sure you have chosen the appropriate fabric, you may want to try a few embroidery stitches on a scrap of the fabric you are going to use to see how they work. Your local craft store may be able to help you choose a fabric if you are unsure.

THREADS

Embroidery threads are available in an array of beautiful colours. I've used stranded embroidery cotton, also known as floss, for all of the designs in this book, and pearl cotton (perle cotton) for finishing. I've also provided colour numbers for DMC thread.

Stranded embroidery floss is a divisible thread made up of six individual strands of mercerized cotton, which can be separated into single strands. These strands can then be used as one, two, three or more strands held together to achieve different effects. For most of these projects, I used two strands; if different, it's indicated in the pattern instructions. Two strands work best for 14-count Aida and linen, and three strands for 11-count Aida.

To separate the strands from the skein, cut an 18in (45cm) length of thread from the skein, hold the thread at the top, and pull the threads out one by one, moving them upwards to avoid tangling. Then, place the threads back together, side by side, before threading into the needle. A longer thread will tangle and knot. You may be tempted to use a longer thread, but 18in (45cm) is perfect.

Pearl cotton is a non-divisible embroidery cotton with a tight twist and a beautiful sheen. It comes in skeins or balls and is only used as a single thread. There are three different sizes available: size 3, 5 and 8. Size 3 is the thickest. In this book, we use pearl cotton (size 5) to gather the back of the fabric in the hoops since it is so strong and holds the fabric securely.

Note: Each skein of thread has its own colour number, and I have listed the colour numbers used for each project. If the suggested thread colour is not available, choose a shade as close as possible to my recommended choice.

HOOPS

Cross stitch can be worked with or without a hoop. I recommend beginners use a hoop. Embroidery hoops come in a wide range of sizes, shapes and materials. They keep the fabric taut and flat as you are working on it so you can keep your stitches even. In this book, we are also using them as frames to display the finished pieces.

A hoop consists of two removable rings held firmly together by a metal screw, which is used to tighten the hoop when the fabric is in place.

I use wooden hoops for my cross stitching, but you can find them in metal and various shades of plastic. They come in sizes from small to large, and round, oval, square or rectangle shapes. Round hoops are the most popular and are what I've chosen for the projects in this book. When stretched in the hoop, the fabric should be firm enough to stitch without puckering or fraying.

YOU WILL ALSO NEED:
- Ruler or tape measure
- Ironing board and iron
- Pressing cloth or clean tea towel
- Sewing thread for basting
- Polyester fibrefill for stuffing pillows and pincushions

CROSS STITCH BASICS

Whether you are brand new to cross stitch or have some experience, these key steps will help you create beautiful projects to gift or keep.

PREPARING YOUR FABRIC

Before beginning to stitch, you may want to prevent the edges of the fabric from fraying. Linen fabric will fray more easily than Aida cloth. You can sew the edges of the fabric with a zig-zag stitch on a sewing machine or oversew around the edge by hand.

POSITIONING THE DESIGN ON THE FABRIC

Firstly, we need to find the centre of the fabric. Fold the fabric gently in half one way, then the other, and baste or tack (sew a line of small running stitches) along the folds so the lines intersect in the centre. This will match with the centre of the chart.

Next, count out from the centre to the number of stitches marked on the chart. Work a row of small running stitches to outline the perimeter of the design. Use a small stitch to mark the top of the design.

If you are using a hoop, centre the design in the hoop (see below for how to put the fabric in the hoop).

READING A CROSS STITCH CHART

The cross stitch chart gives you all the information you need to copy the design from the symbols on the chart to the weave of the fabric. Each coloured square on the chart represents one cross stitch on the fabric. Each colour on the chart represents the same colour of stranded cotton. The charts have arrows that indicate the centre. The chart is your map to stitching.

PUTTING THE FABRIC IN THE HOOP

After finding the centre of the fabric, you are ready to place it into the hoop.

1. First, loosen the metal screw on the hoop. You will now have two rings: a smaller inner ring and a slightly larger outer ring. Place the inner ring under the fabric, centring the design.

1

2. Push the outer ring over the inner ring, keeping the screw at the top of the hoop. Tighten the screw, pulling the edges of the fabric a little to get it taut. When the design is centred, you are ready to stitch.

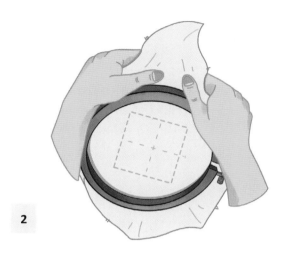

2

BEGINNING TO STITCH

Cut an 18in (45cm) length of embroidery thread. See page 8 for separating the strands. Thread the needle, using a needle threader if necessary.

To begin a stitch, the thread needs to be secured in some way. I use an 'away knot' on the front of the work. An away knot is worked a few inches away from the area where the embroidery begins. To begin, tie a knot at the end of the thread and take the needle down through the front of the fabric to the back, 3in (7.6cm) to the right of the position of your first stitch. This long thread will be stitched over and held in place by the cross stitches.

When you reach the knot, check that the thread is covered on the wrong side, then cut off the knot. Try to keep the wrong side as tidy as possible.

When you have finished using a colour, or your thread is too short to continue, finish the thread by taking it to the wrong side and running it under some worked stitches for about 1in (2.5cm), then cut.

To start a new thread, either use an away knot or slip the new thread under the worked stitches on the wrong side.

Some people begin stitching by following the chart from the centre stitch. I prefer to begin at the top left-hand corner and work down in rows. Start where you feel the most comfortable. Follow the chart, remembering that each square represents one stitch and one colour, and empty squares have no stitches so the fabric background shows through.

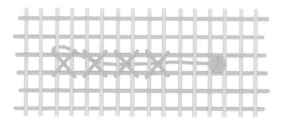

WORKING A CROSS STITCH

A cross stitch is formed by two stitches crossing each other to create an X, and they are usually worked in rows from left to right in one direction, working one half of the stitch, sloping from left to right. Then, the stitches are completed, coming back across the row from top to bottom, forming a cross. Always make sure the top stitches slope in the same direction.

1. Working from left to right, bring your needle up at A and down at B. If you are working a row of cross stitches, continue working slanted stitches evenly in this manner.

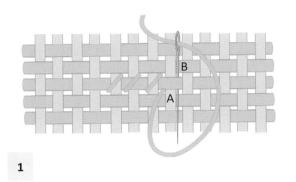

1

2. On the return, work from right to left, crossing over the first stitches from C to D, forming a cross. To end the stitch, go down through the fabric to the wrong side at D.

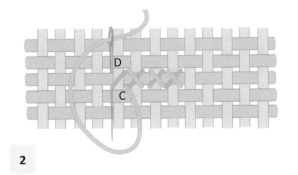

2

RUNNING STITCH

This is also called a tacking or basting stitch. If you know how to hand sew, you know how to do a running stitch. Running stitches are used to mark the centre and outline the size of the stitched area.

Working from right to left, bring the needle up at A, down at B, and out at C. Continue in this manner, spacing the stitches evenly. To end the stitch, go down through the fabric to the wrong side at B.

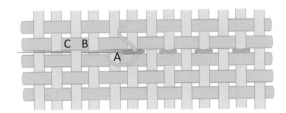

BACKSTITCH

This stitch is used to outline the cross stitches or add details. They are used anywhere you need to 'draw' with thread. Backstitches are worked after all the cross stitches are completed using one or two strands of thread. This will be indicated in each design.

Working from right to left, bring the needle up at A and make a small backwards stitch by going down at B. Bring the needle through at C. Move the needle to the left under the fabric. Continue this pattern, bringing the needle up a space ahead and down into the hole made by the last stitch. To end the stitch, go down through the fabric to the wrong side at C.

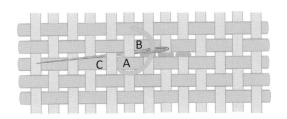

FRENCH KNOT

The French knot is used to create individual elements, such as eyes, and to add detail and texture. The basic French knot is wrapped once, but you can wrap it twice, three or even four times to create a larger knot. The number of wraps will be indicated in each design.

1. Bring needle up at A and twist through the thread, then bring it over the needle.

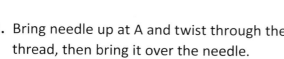

1

A

2. Pull the needle up over the thread and back down into A.

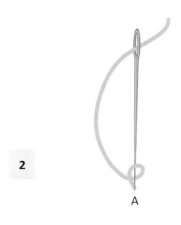

2

A

3. You are essentially tying a knot with the needle and thread. For a French knot wrapped twice, twist the thread over the needle twice in Step 1.

3

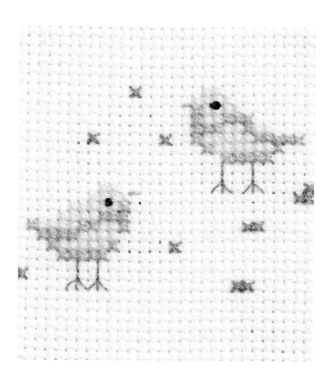

FINISHING

When you're done stitching your piece, take the time to finish it neatly. Make sure your threads are all woven in on the back and trimmed. Remove the basting threads. If necessary, you might like to wash it gently and dry it flat on a towel with the right side facing up. Try not to crumple the fabric during washing as this will create creases.

Lay the fabric wrong side up on an ironing board or padded surface, place a pressing cloth on top and gently iron.

FINISHING PIECES IN A HOOP

If you want to use the hoop as a frame for your work, you'll want to cover the back of your stitching so it does not show. I do a gathered finish and add a felt backing.

1. With a long length of pearl cotton and the wrong side facing, insert the needle into the fabric about ½in (1.3cm) from the outer edge of the hoop. Secure with several double stitches. Work a circle of running stitches around the perimeter of the hoop. Leave a long tail.

2. Using embroidery scissors, trim off excess fabric at least ½in (1.3cm) away from the running stitches. Gather the running stitches by pulling the pearl cotton thread until the fabric fits snugly around the inner hoop, then secure the thread with a few double stitches.

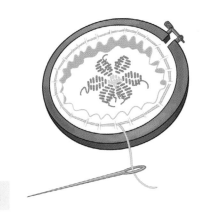

2

3. Place the felt backing on top of the fabric. Then, using pearl cotton, stitch through both the felt and fabric to attach the backing.

3

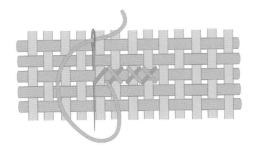

1

FRAMING CROSS STITCH

Using a purchased frame is an easy way to showcase your stitchery. When choosing a frame, be sure there is enough space in the opening to fit all the stitches, but also ensure that it's not too big and swamps a small motif. Different brands of fabric vary in stiffness. If your fabric is soft, press it with spray starch to give it some body.

Disassemble the frame, remove the glass and discard safely. If your frame comes with a mat (a piece of white backing cardboard the size of the inside of the frame), place the mat over the motif, centring it. Pull the fabric taut and make sure the lines of the Aida cloth are straight. Mark around the outer edge of the mat with a pencil. Cut along the lines so the fabric is the same size as the mat. Using double-sided tape, mount the cross stitch to the back of the mat. If the frame does not come with a mat, you will need to cut one from white card to place behind the stitchery.

Alternatively, you can use acid-free, self-stick mounting board and position the cross stitch on it, centring the motif. Be sure the Aida threads are straight. Trim to fit and place in the frame.

If you are uncomfortable with framing, or you need a custom-cut mat or frame, try your local framing store.

OTHER PROJECTS

Cross stitch can be finished in many different ways and made into many different items. Follow the individual instructions throughout the book for creating the projects shown.

DOWN ON THE FARM

SKILL LEVEL: EASY

Farmhouse-style decor is very popular, and these delightful motifs mounted in a rustic frame make the perfect addition to a country-style home.

YOU WILL NEED

MATERIALS
For each motif
- 11-count white Aida fabric, three pieces measuring 6 x 8in (15 x 20.5cm)
- Basting thread
- One 9¾ x 16½in (25 x 42cm) frame with three 4 x 6in (10 x 15cm) openings
- Tapestry needle, no. 24
- Scissors
- Double-sided tape

THREADS
DMC six-strand embroidery thread, one skein of each:
Red Hen
817 Very Dark Coral Red
922 Light Copper
402 Very Light Mahogany
945 Tawny
742 Light Tangerine

Blue Truck
B5200 Snow White
606 Bright Orange Red
301 Medium Mahogany
798 Dark Delft Blue
648 Light Beaver Grey
809 Delft Blue
676 Light Old Gold
310 Black

Green Tractor
436 Tan
310 Black
702 Kelly Green
648 Light Beaver Grey
740 Tangerine
676 Light Old Gold
021 Light Alizarin

TIP
Try stitching the truck or tractor design in three different colours for your farming friends.

METHOD

Read the instructions for preparing the fabric and marking the centre on page 10. Following the chart and colour key, begin stitching at the centre over one square of Aida fabric using three strands of thread.

Red Hen: Work a French knot using two strands of 742, wrapping twice for the eye.

Blue Truck: Work backstitches using one strand of 310 thread.

Green Tractor: Work backstitches using two strands of 702.

Stitching area Red Hen
32 x 26 sts, 3 x 2½in (7.5 x 6.5cm)
Stitching area Blue Truck
47 x 25 sts, 4¼ x 2¼in (10.5 x 5.5cm)
Stitching area Green Tractor
53 x 22 sts, 4¾ x 2in (12 x 5cm)

FINISHING

Remove basting threads. Press lightly from the wrong side on a padded surface. See framing instructions on page 15.

RED HEN

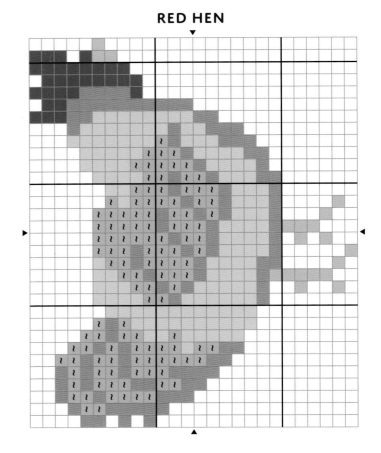

KEY

	NO STITCH
	817 VERY DARK CORAL RED
	922 LIGHT COPPER
~	402 VERY LIGHT MAHOGANY
	945 TAWNY
	742 LIGHT TANGERINE

BLUE TRUCK

GREEN TRACTOR

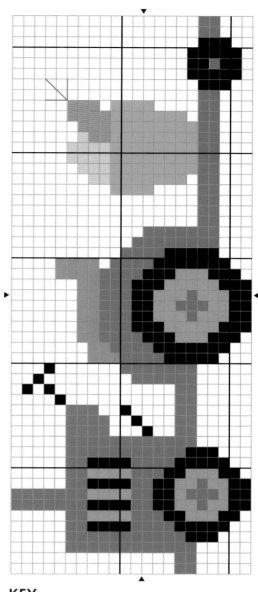

KEY

☐ NO STITCH

• B5200 SNOW WHITE

■ 606 BRIGHT ORANGE RED

■ 301 MEDIUM MAHOGANY

■ 798 DARK DELFT BLUE

■ 648 LIGHT BEAVER GREY

■ 809 DELFT BLUE

■ 676 LIGHT OLD GOLD

■ 310 BLACK

KEY

☐ NO STITCH

■ 436 TAN

■ 310 BLACK

■ 702 KELLY GREEN

■ 648 LIGHT BEAVER GREY

■ 740 TANGERINE

■ 676 LIGHT OLD GOLD

■ 021 LIGHT ALIZARIN

PATCHWORK PINCUSHION

SKILL LEVEL: EASY

This makes a quick and easy gift that will be loved by your quilting friends.

YOU WILL NEED

MATERIALS
- 14-count white Aida fabric, two pieces measuring 7 x 7in (18 x 18cm)
- Basting thread
- 4in (10cm) hoop
- One small white 4-hole button
- Tapestry needle, no. 24
- Sewing needle and thread or sewing machine
- Small amount of fibrefill for stuffing
- Scissors

THREADS
DMC six-strand embroidery thread, one skein of each:
349 Dark Coral
B5200 Snow White
798 Dark Delft Blue
799 Medium Delft Blue

METHOD
Read the instructions for preparing the fabric and marking the centre on page 10, then baste the Aida. Following the chart and colour key, begin stitching at the centre over one square of the Aida using two strands of thread. Stitching area: 45 x 45 sts, 3¼ x 3¼in (8 x 8cm).

FINISHING
Remove basting threads. Press lightly on the wrong side on a padded surface. Place the unstitched piece of Aida fabric over the cross-stitched motif with right sides together. Baste a line one square away from the 3in (7.5cm) square cross stitch area. Machine stitch or use tiny backstitches to sew around three sides, and ½in (1.3cm) in at each end of the fourth side. Remove the basting thread and trim the excess fabric to ½in (1.3cm) from the seams. Trim across corners. Turn the piece to the right side, square out the corners, stuff and hand sew the fourth side closed. Sew the button in the middle of the centre quilt block, sewing through the stuffing and backing and pulling tightly to create a pillow effect. Secure thread.

PATCHWORK PINCUSHION

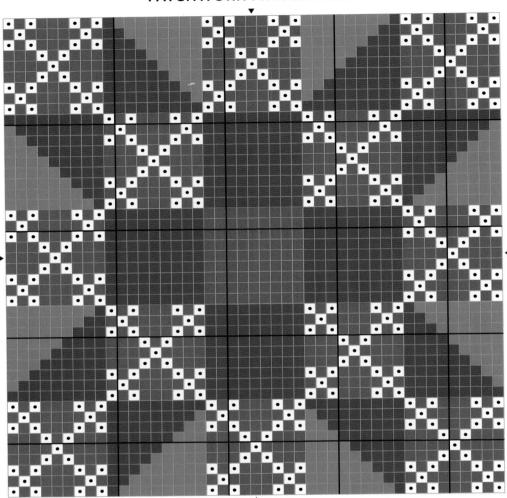

KEY

☐	NO STITCH
■	349 DARK CORAL
•	B5200 SNOW WHITE
■	798 DARK DELFT BLUE
■	799 MEDIUM DELFT BLUE

JAR PINCUSHION

SKILL LEVEL: EASY

This decorative jar becomes a perfect holder for threads, needles, buttons and other needlework supplies.

YOU WILL NEED

MATERIALS

- 14-count white Aida fabric, one piece measuring 7 x 7in (18 x 18cm)
- 3¼in (8cm) wide-mouth preserving jar
- Basting thread
- Tapestry needle, no. 24
- Small amount of fibrefill for stuffing
- Scissors

THREADS

DMC six-strand embroidery thread, one skein of each:

813 Light Blue
817 Red
436 Tan
970 Light Pumpkin
310 Black

For finishing:

DMC pearl cotton #5 White

METHOD

Read the instructions for preparing the fabric and marking the centre on page 10. Following the chart and colour key, begin stitching at the centre over one square of Aida fabric using two strands of thread. Work backstitches using one strand of 310 and 813. Stitching area: 26 x 30 sts, 2 x 2¼in (5 x 5.5cm).

FINISHING

Press lightly on the wrong side on a padded surface. Use a plate or cup as a guide to mark a circle ½in (1.3cm) in from the edge of the fabric. Cut around the marked circle. Using pearl cotton, make a running stitch ½in (1.3cm) in from the edge. Gather slightly, insert fibrefill and the flat lid, and pull to gather the fabric tightly, making sure the motif is centred. Fasten securely. Place the cushion on top of the jar and attach using the ring.

JAR PINCUSHION

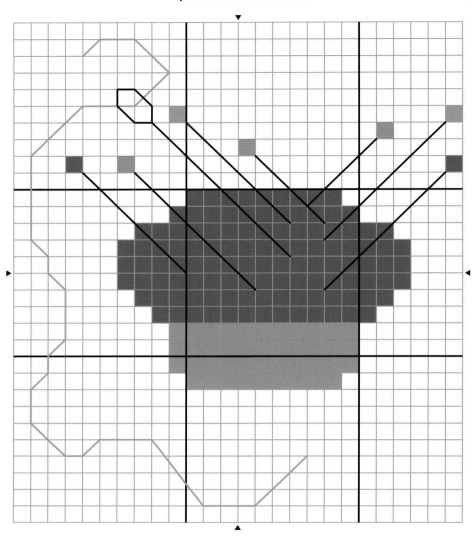

KEY

	NO STITCH
	813 LIGHT BLUE
	817 RED
	436 TAN
	970 LIGHT PUMPKIN
	310 BLACK

BEE CUSHION

SKILL LEVEL: EASY

This whimsical cushion celebrates bees and how important they are to our environment.

YOU WILL NEED

MATERIALS
- 11-count ivory Aida fabric, one piece measuring 16 x 16in (40.5 x 40.5cm)
- White cotton fabric 16 x 16in (40.5 x 40.5cm) for cushion backing
- 12 x 12in (30.5 x 30.5cm) cushion insert
- Basting thread
- Tapestry needle, no. 24
- Sewing needle and thread or sewing machine
- Scissors

THREADS
DMC six-strand embroidery thread,
one skein of each:
310 Black
001 White Tin
740 Tangerine
780 Light Topaz
726 Topaz
3822 Light Straw
729 Medium Old Gold
437 Light Tan

METHOD
Read the instructions for preparing fabric and marking the centre on page 10. Following the chart and colour key, begin stitching at the centre over one square of Aida fabric using three strands of thread.

Work backstitches using one strand of 310 for inside the bee's wings and two strands for the remaining stitches; use two strands of 780 for the beehive. Stitching area: 89 x 81 sts, 8 x 7¾in (20.5 x 19.5cm).

FINISHING

Remove basting threads. Press lightly from the wrong side on a padded surface. Baste a 12in (30.5cm) square (this will be the finished size of the cushion) centred around the 8in (20.5cm) stitched area. Place the cotton backing over the cross stitch piece with right sides together. Following the basting line on the Aida fabric, baste the cushion back and cross-stitched pieces together.

Machine stitch or use tiny backstitches to sew around three sides, and 2in (5cm) in from each end of the fourth side. Remove tacking thread, then trim any excess fabric away to ½in (1.3cm) from the seams. Trim across corners. Turn to the right side, square out the corners and press. Place cushion insert inside and hand sew the fourth side closed.

BEE CUSHION

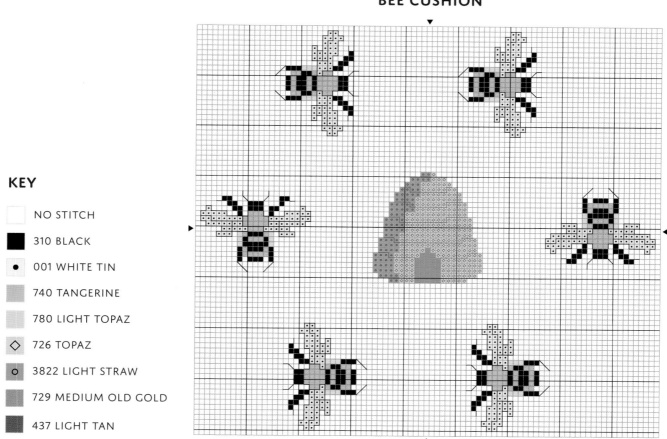

KEY

⬜	NO STITCH
⬛	310 BLACK
•	001 WHITE TIN
	740 TANGERINE
	780 LIGHT TOPAZ
◇	726 TOPAZ
○	3822 LIGHT STRAW
	729 MEDIUM OLD GOLD
	437 LIGHT TAN

BIRDHOUSE BRANCH

FABRIC 14-count white Aida fabric, one piece measuring 8 x 8in (20.5 x 20.5cm)
THREADS DMC six-strand embroidery thread, one skein of each colour listed
HOOP 4in (10cm)
STITCHING AREA 36 x 30 sts, 2½ x 2in (6.5 x 5cm)

Read the instructions for preparing fabric and marking the centre on page 10. Following the chart and colour key, begin stitching at the centre over one square of Aida fabric using two strands of thread. Work backstitches using one strand of 310 thread.

BLUE BICYCLE

FABRIC 14-count white Aida fabric, one piece measuring 8 x 8in (20.5 x 20.5cm)
THREADS DMC six-strand embroidery thread, one skein of each colour listed
HOOP 4in (10cm)
STITCHING AREA 28 x 46 sts, 2 x 3in (5 x 7.5cm)

Read the instructions for preparing fabric and marking the centre on page 10. Following the chart and colour key, start stitching at the centre over one square of Aida fabric using two strands of thread. Work backstitches using one strand of 414 thread.

BIRDHOUSE BRANCH

KEY

	NO STITCH
	703 CHARTREUSE
	817 VERY DARK CORAL RED
	972 DEEP CANARY
	813 LIGHT BLUE
	008 DARK DRIFTWOOD
	310 BLACK
	033 FUCHSIA

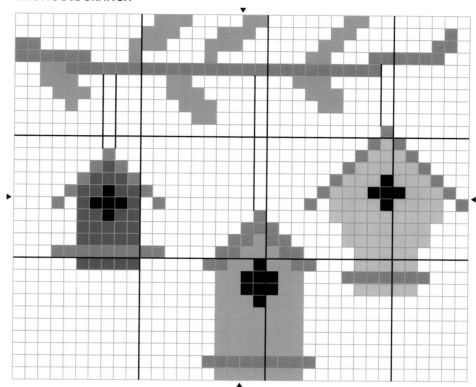

BLUE BICYCLE

KEY

	NO STITCH
	704 BRIGHT CHARTREUSE
	334 MEDIUM BABY BLUE
	402 VERY LIGHT MAHOGANY
	718 PLUM
	800 PALE DELFT BLUE
	957 PALE GERANIUM
	414 DARK STEEL GREY
	310 BLACK

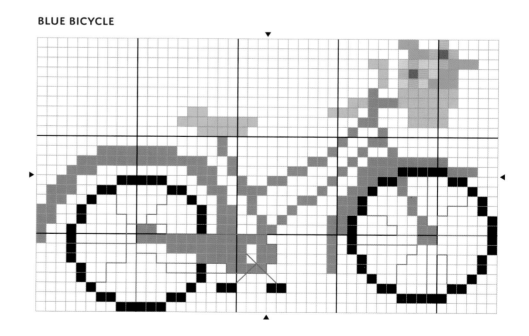

BUZZING BEE

FABRIC 14-count white Aida fabric, one piece measuring 7 x 7in (18 x 18cm)
THREADS DMC six-strand embroidery thread, one skein of each colour listed
HOOP 3in (7.5cm)
STITCHING AREA 23 x 18 sts, 1½ x 1¼in (4 x 3cm)

Read the instructions for preparing the fabric and marking the centre on page 10. Following the chart and colour key, begin stitching at the centre over one square of Aida fabric using two strands of thread. Work backstitches on the wing using one strand of 310 and remaining backstitches using two strands of 310 thread.

STRAWBERRY PINCUSHION

FABRIC 14-count white Aida fabric, one piece measuring 7 x 7in (18 x 18cm)
THREADS DMC six-strand embroidery thread, one skein of each colour listed
HOOP 3in (7.5cm)
STITCHING AREA 32 x 19 sts, 2¼ x 1¼in (5.5 x 3cm)

Read the instructions for preparing the fabric and marking the centre on page 10. Following the chart and colour key, begin stitching at the centre over one square of Aida fabric using two strands of thread. Work backstitches using two strands of 310 thread.

BUZZING BEE

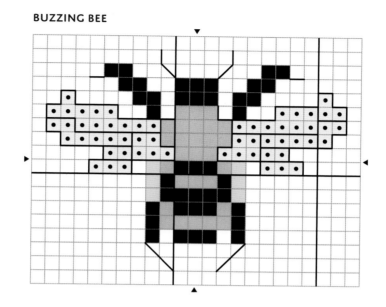

KEY

□	NO STITCH
■	310 BLACK
•	001 WHITE TIN
▨	742 LIGHT TANGERINE
▨	726 LIGHT TOPAZ

STRAWBERRY PINCUSHION

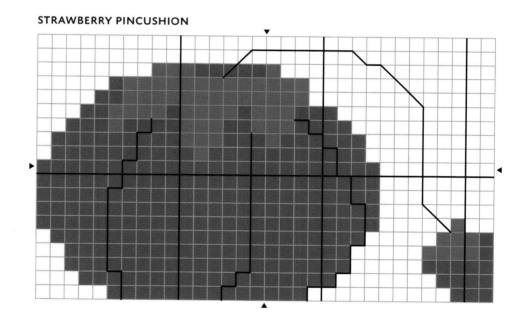

KEY

□	NO STITCH
▨	817 GARNET
▨	905 DARK PARROT GREEN
■	310 BLACK

WASHING DAY

FABRIC 14-count pale blue Aida fabric, one piece measuring 8 x 8in (20.5 x 20.5cm)
THREADS DMC six-strand embroidery thread, one skein of each colour listed
HOOP 4in (10cm)
STITCHING AREA 48 x 40 sts, 3½ x 3in (9 x 7.5cm)

Read the instructions for preparing the fabric and marking the centre on page 10. Following the chart and colour key, start stitching at the centre over one square of Aida fabric using two strands of thread. Work backstitches using two strands of 310 thread.

BUSY BEEHIVE

FABRIC 14-count pale blue Aida fabric, one piece measuring 7 x 7in (18 x 18cm)
THREADS DMC six-strand embroidery thread, one skein of each colour listed
HOOP 3in (7.5cm)
STITCHING AREA 26 x 25 sts, 1¾ x 1¾in (4.5 x 4.5cm)

Read the instructions for preparing the fabric and marking the centre on page 10. Following the chart and colour key, start stitching at the centre over one square of Aida fabric using two strands of thread. Work backstitches using two strands of 310 thread and two strands of 780 thread.

WASHING DAY

KEY

☐ NO STITCH
■ 310 BLACK
▨ 155 FORGET-ME-NOT BLUE
⊡ 333 VERY DARK BLUE VIOLET
▨ 964 LIGHT SEA GREEN
▨ 943 MEDIUM AQUAMARINE
▨ 950 LIGHT DESERT SAND
▨ 3328 DARK SALMON

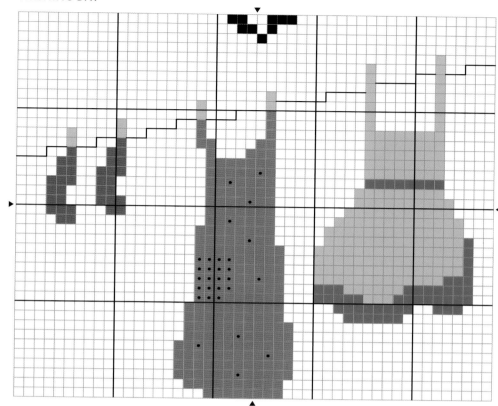

BUSY BEEHIVE

KEY

☐ NO STITCH
▨ 3822 LIGHT STRAW
⊙ 729 MEDIUM OLD GOLD
▨ 436 TAN
■ 310 BLACK
• B5200 SNOW WHITE
▨ 780 ULTRA VERY DARK TOPAZ

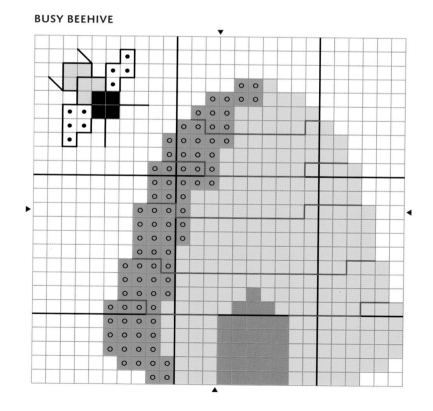

SEWING MACHINE

FABRIC 14-count white Aida fabric, one piece measuring 9 x 9in (23 x 23cm)
THREADS DMC six-strand embroidery thread, one skein of each colour listed
HOOP 5in (12.5cm)
STITCHING AREA 51 x 37 sts, 3½ x 2½in (9 x 6.5cm)

Read the instructions for preparing fabric and marking the centre on page 10. Following the chart and colour key, start stitching at the centre over one square of Aida fabric using two strands of thread. Work backstitches using one strand of 413 and one strand of 825 thread.

CHIRPING CHICKS

FABRIC 14-count white Aida fabric, one piece measuring 7 x 7in (18 x 18cm)
THREADS DMC six-strand embroidery thread, one skein of each colour listed
HOOP 3in (7.5cm)
STITCHING AREA 30 x 21 sts, 2¼ x 1½in (5.5 x 3cm)

Read the instructions for preparing the fabric and marking the centre on page 10. Following the chart and colour key, start stitching at the centre over one square of Aida fabric using two strands of thread. Work backstitches using one strand of 420 thread, then French knot for the chick's eye using two strands of 310 thread wrapped twice.

SEWING MACHINE

KEY

☐	NO STITCH
■	413 DARK PEWTER GREY
■	415 PEARL GREY
■	970 LIGHT PUMPKIN
■	743 MEDIUM YELLOW
■	825 DARK BLUE
■	794 LIGHT CORNFLOWER BLUE
■	407 DARK DESERT SAND
■	950 LIGHT DESERT SAND

CHIRPING CHICKS

KEY

☐	NO STITCH
■	310 BLACK
■	783 MEDIUM TOPAZ
■	744 PALE YELLOW
■	420 DARK HAZELNUT BROWN

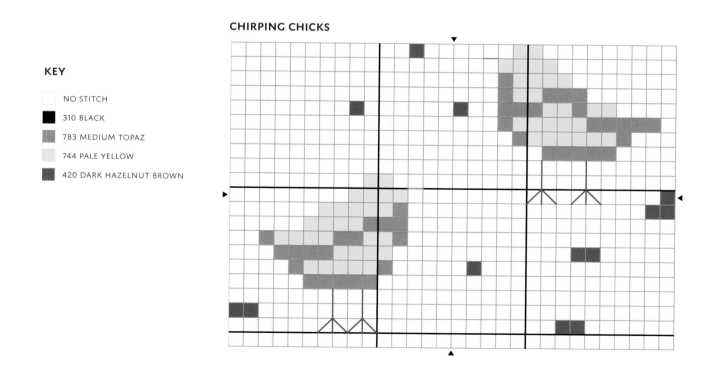

COASTAL CARAVAN

FABRIC 14-count white Aida fabric, one piece measuring 10 x 10in (25.5 x 25.5cm)
THREADS DMC six-strand embroidery thread, one skein of each colour listed
HOOP 6in (15.5cm)
STITCHING AREA 61 x 41 sts, 4½ x 3in (11.5 x 7.5cm)

Read the instructions for preparing the fabric and marking the centre on page 10. Following the chart and colour key, start stitching at the centre over one square of Aida fabric using two strands of thread.

COUNTRY CARAVAN

FABRIC 14-count white Aida fabric, one piece measuring 9 x 9in (23 x 23cm)
THREADS DMC six-strand embroidery thread, one skein of each colour listed
HOOP 5in (12.5cm)
STITCHING AREA 63 x 43 sts, 4½ x 3in (11.5 x 7.5cm)

Read the instructions for preparing the fabric and marking the centre on page 10. Following the chart and colour key, start stitching at the centre over one square of Aida fabric using two strands of thread. Work backstitches using two strands of 310 thread.

COASTAL CARAVAN

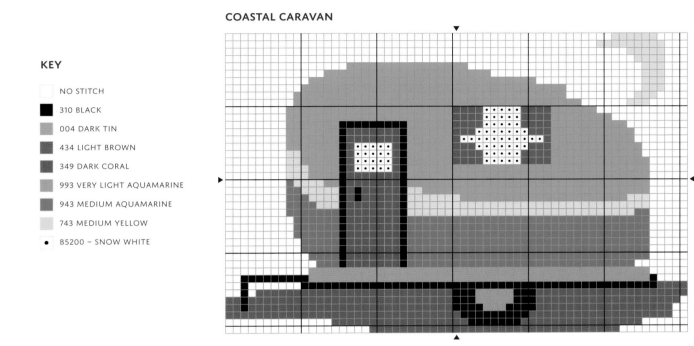

KEY

☐	NO STITCH
■	310 BLACK
▨	004 DARK TIN
▨	434 LIGHT BROWN
▨	349 DARK CORAL
▨	993 VERY LIGHT AQUAMARINE
▨	943 MEDIUM AQUAMARINE
▨	743 MEDIUM YELLOW
•	B5200 – SNOW WHITE

COUNTRY CARAVAN

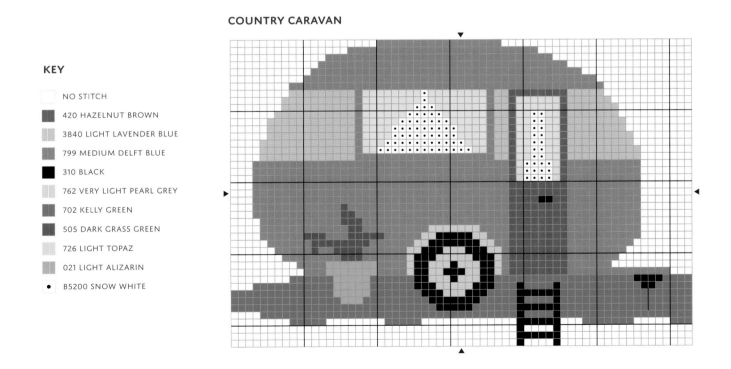

KEY

☐	NO STITCH
▨	420 HAZELNUT BROWN
▨	3840 LIGHT LAVENDER BLUE
▨	799 MEDIUM DELFT BLUE
■	310 BLACK
▨	762 VERY LIGHT PEARL GREY
▨	702 KELLY GREEN
▨	505 DARK GRASS GREEN
▨	726 LIGHT TOPAZ
▨	021 LIGHT ALIZARIN
•	B5200 SNOW WHITE

BLACK CAT

FABRIC 14-count white Aida fabric, one piece measuring 9 x 9in (23 x 23cm)
THREADS DMC six-strand embroidery thread, one skein of each colour listed
HOOP 5in (12.5cm)
STITCHING AREA 51 x 45 sts, 3½ x 3¼in (9 x 8cm)

Read the instructions for preparing the fabric and marking the centre on page 10. Following the chart and colour key, start stitching at the centre over one square of Aida fabric using two strands of thread. Work backstitches using one strand of 310 thread. For the cat's whiskers, straight stitch using one strand of B5200.

STAR QUILT

FABRIC 14-count white Aida fabric, one piece measuring 9 x 9in (23 x 23cm)
THREADS DMC six-strand embroidery thread, one skein of each colour listed
HOOP 5in (12.5cm)
STITCHING AREA 39 x 39 sts, 2¾ x 2¾in (7 x 7cm)

Read the instructions for preparing the fabric and marking the centre on page 10. Following the chart and colour key, start stitching at the centre over one square of Aida fabric using two strands of thread. Reposition motif so it is on a diagonal.

BLACK CAT

KEY

☐ NO STITCH

■ 310 BLACK

● B5200 SNOW WHITE

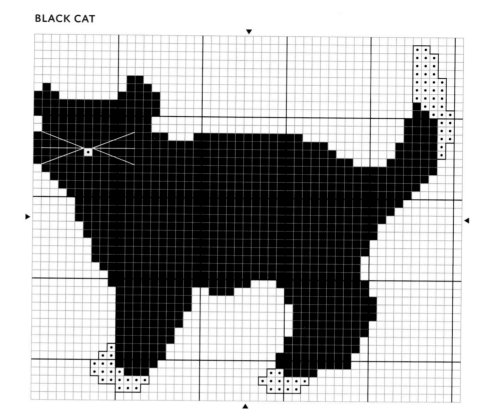

STAR QUILT

KEY

☐ NO STITCH

■ 792 DARK CORNFLOWER BLUE

▨ 3840 LIGHT LAVENDER BLUE

▨ 3855 LIGHT AUTUMN GOLD

☐ 3823 ULTRA PALE YELLOW

■ 943 MEDIUM AQUAMARINE

■ 959 MEDIUM SEA GREEN

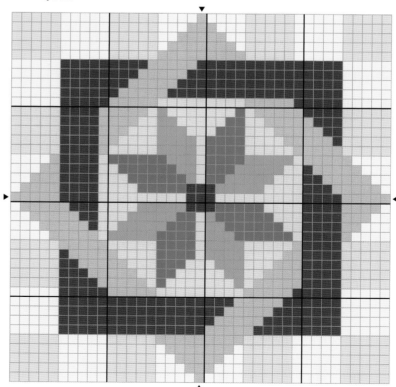

BEACH DAY

FABRIC 14-count white Aida fabric, one piece measuring 9 x 9in (23 x 23cm)
THREADS DMC six-strand embroidery thread, one skein of each colour listed
HOOP 5in (12.5cm)
STITCHING AREA 54 x 54 sts, 3¾ x 3¾in (9.5 x 9.5cm)

Read the instructions for preparing the fabric and marking the centre on page 10. Following the chart and colour key, start stitching at the centre over one square of Aida fabric using two strands of thread. Work backstitches using one strand of 310 thread.

MYSTICAL MANDALA

FABRIC 14-count white Aida fabric, one piece measuring 8 x 8in (20.5 x 20.5cm)
THREADS DMC six-strand embroidery thread, one skein of each colour listed
HOOP 4in (10cm)
STITCHING AREA 44 x 44 sts, 3 x 3in (7.5 x 7.5cm)

Read the instructions for preparing the fabric and marking the centre on page 10. Following the chart and colour key, start stitching at the centre over one square of Aida fabric using two strands of thread.

BEACH DAY

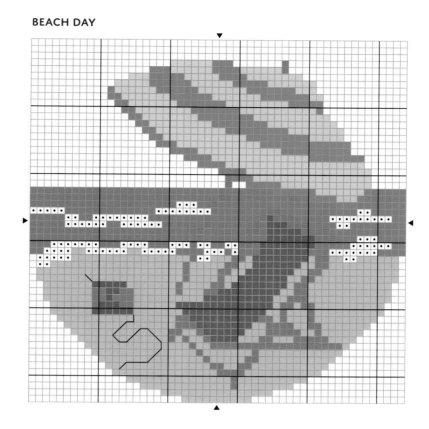

KEY

	NO STITCH
	958 DARK SEA GREEN
	973 BRIGHT CANARY
	407 DARK DESERT SAND
	606 BRIGHT ORANGE RED
	950 LIGHT DESERT SAND
	310 BLACK
•	B5200 SNOW WHITE
	807 PEACOCK BLUE

MYSTICAL MANDALA

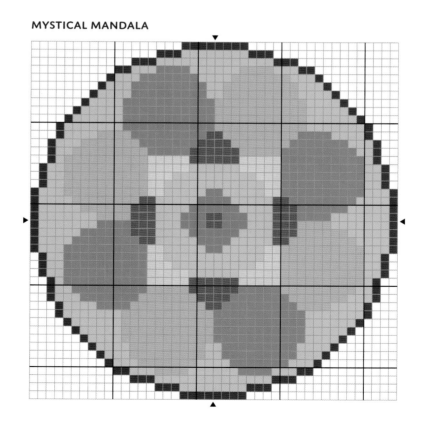

KEY

	NO STITCH
	824 VERY DARK BLUE
	793 MEDIUM CORNFLOWER BLUE
	794 LIGHT CORNFLOWER BLUE
	964 LIGHT SEA GREEN
	958 DARK SEA GREEN
	553 VIOLET
	153 LILAC

ADIRONDACK CHAIR

FABRIC 14-count white Aida fabric, one piece measuring 8 x 8in (20.5 x 20.5cm)
THREADS DMC six-strand embroidery thread, one skein of each colour listed
HOOP 4in (10cm)
STITCHING AREA 38 x 36 sts, 2¾ x 2½in (7 x 6.5cm)

Read the instructions for preparing the fabric and marking the centre on page 10. Following the chart and colour key, start stitching at the centre over one square of Aida fabric using two strands of thread.

FLOWER MANDALA

FABRIC 14-count white Aida fabric, one piece measuring 8 x 8in (20.5 x 20.5cm)
THREADS DMC six-strand embroidery thread, one skein of each colour listed
HOOP 4in (10cm)
STITCHING AREA 42 x 42 sts, 3 x 3in (7.5 x 7.5cm)

Read the instructions for preparing the fabric and marking the centre on page 10. Following the chart and colour key, start stitching at the centre over one square of Aida fabric using two strands of thread.

ADIRONDACK CHAIR

KEY

KEY

- NO STITCH
- 414 DARK STEEL GREY
- 415 PEARL GREY
- 827 VERY LIGHT BLUE
- 518 LIGHT WEDGEWOOD
- • B5200 SNOW WHITE
- 945 TAWNY
- 436 TAN
- 958 DARK SEA GREEN

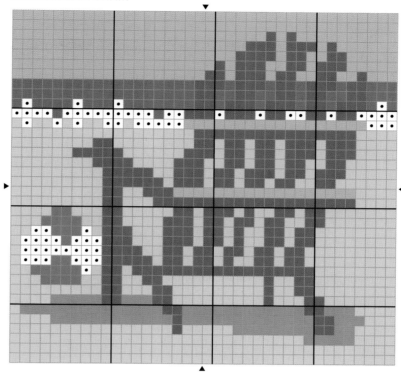

FLOWER MANDALA

KEY

- NO STITCH
- 013 MEDIUM LIGHT NILE GREEN
- 703 CHARTREUSE
- 824 VERY DARK BLUE
- 3840 LIGHT LAVENDER BLUE
- 3760 MEDIUM WEDGEWOOD
- 033 FUCHSIA
- 3836 LIGHT GRAPE
- 3825 PALE PUMPKIN
- 721 MEDIUM ORANGE SPICE

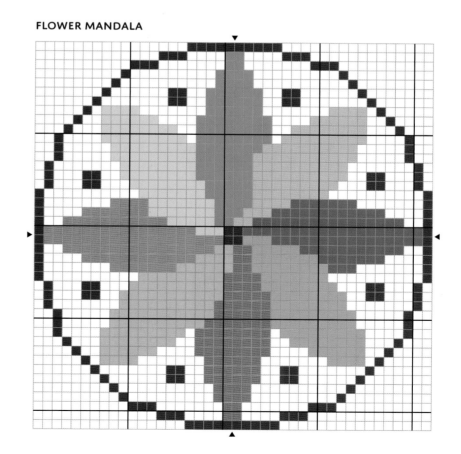

STRAW HAT

FABRIC 14-count white Aida fabric, one piece measuring 8 x 8in (20.5 x 20.5cm)
THREADS DMC six-strand embroidery thread, one skein of each colour listed
HOOP 4in (10cm)
STITCHING AREA 50 x 22 sts, 3½ x 1½in (9 x 4cm)

Read the instructions for preparing the fabric and marking the centre on page 10. Following the chart and colour key, start stitching at the centre over one square of Aida fabric using two strands of thread.

STRAW HAT

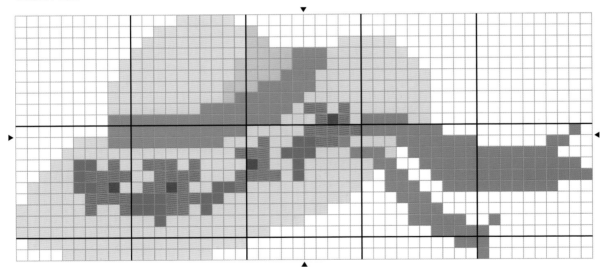

KEY

☐	NO STITCH
■	702 KELLY GREEN
☐	677 VERY LIGHT OLD GOLD
☐	676 LIGHT OLD GOLD
■	3843 ELECTRIC BLUE
■	603 CRANBERRY
■	900 DARK BURNT ORANGE

CONE SHELL PHOTO ALBUM

SKILL LEVEL: EASY

This is a delightful choice to decorate a photo album holding memories of a summer holiday.

YOU WILL NEED

MATERIALS

- 14-count white Aida fabric, one piece measuring 8 x 8in (20.5 x 20.5cm)
- Basting thread
- Cloth-covered photo album with 3½ x 3½in (9 x 9cm) window
- Tapestry needle, no. 24
- Scissors
- Double-sided tape

THREADS

DMC six-strand embroidery thread, one skein of each:
951 Brown
224 Pink
799 Medium Delft Blue

METHOD

Read the instructions for preparing the fabric and marking the centre on page 10. Following the chart and colour key, begin stitching at the centre over one square of Aida fabric using two strands of thread. Stitching area: 32 x 40 sts, 2¼ x 2¾in (5.5 x 7cm).

FINISHING

Remove basting threads. Press lightly from the wrong side on a padded surface. Centre the shell inside the album window, then trim away any excess fabric leaving at least ½in (1.3cm) for mounting. Use double-sided tape to secure in place.

TIP

Take care that the embroidered area is perfectly centred in the window before trimming the excess fabric.

CONE SHELL PHOTO ALBUM

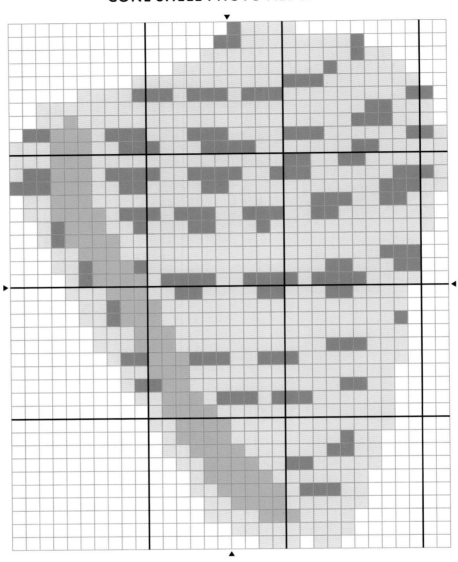

KEY

	NO STITCH
	951 BROWN
	224 PINK
	799 BLUE

SNOWDROP SACHET

SKILL LEVEL: INTERMEDIATE

Beautiful snowdrops stitched on fine linen are the perfect motif for a decorative sachet. Hang it on a door handle, from a cupboard doorknob or in a bathroom.

YOU WILL NEED

MATERIALS

- 28-count white even-weave linen, two pieces measuring 7 x 7in (18 x 18cm)
- Basting thread
- Approx. 1yd (1m) of white satin ribbon ¼in (5mm) wide
- Tapestry needle, no. 24
- Sewing needle and thread or sewing machine
- Small amount of fibrefill (or potpourri sachet) for stuffing
- Scissors

THREADS

DMC six-strand embroidery thread, one skein of each:
B5200 Snow White
503 Light Blue Green
535 Very Light Ash Grey
522 Fern Green
501 Dark Blue Green

METHOD

Read the instructions for preparing the fabric and marking the centre on page 10. Following the chart and colour key, begin stitching at the centre over two fabric threads (page 10) of the linen fabric using two strands of thread. Stitching area: 45 x 54 sts, 3¼ x 3¾in (8 x 9.5cm). Work backstitches using one strand of 535.

TIP
If using lavender or potpourri, it must be contained in a small fabric sachet that is slightly smaller than the stitched sachet.

FINISHING

Remove basting threads. Press lightly on the wrong side on a padded surface. Using small basting stitches, baste eight threads away from the cross-stitched area on three sides, and 28 threads on the fourth side for the top. This represents the finished size. Place the cross-stitched piece on top of the unstitched piece of linen with right sides together. Following the basting lines on the cross-stitched piece, baste the two pieces together on three sides, leaving the top open. Machine or hand stitch along the basting lines. Trim excess fabric to ½in (1.3cm)

from the seams; leave approx. ¾in (1.5cm) above the basting line at the top edge. Trim across corners, turn to the right side, square out the corners and press. Stuff with fibrefill or a potpourri sachet. Press the seam allowance to the inside at the top and sew closed along the basting line. Tie a bow at one end of the ribbon, secure the other end of the ribbon to the back of the bow to form a loop, and then sew it to the centre top of the sachet.

SNOWDROP SACHET

KEY

- NO STITCH
- • B5200 SNOW WHITE
- 503 LIGHT BLUE GREEN
- 535 VERY LIGHT ASH GREY
- 522 FERN GREEN
- 501 DARK BLUE GREEN

POTPOURRI SACHETS

SKILL LEVEL: INTERMEDIATE

*Forget-Me-Not and Queen Anne's lace are reminders of a beautiful garden in spring.
Stitched onto these linen sachets, you can appreciate their floral beauty all year round.*

YOU WILL NEED

MATERIALS
For each sachet
- 28-count white even-weave linen, two pieces measuring 7 x 7in (18 x 18cm)
- Basting thread
- Approx. 0.75yd (60cm) each of blue and lavender satin ribbon ½in (1.3cm) wide
- Tapestry needle, no. 24
- Sewing needle and thread or sewing machine
- Small amount of dried lavender
- Two pieces 6 x 6in (15 x 15cm) cotton fabric for the lavender bag
- Scissors

THREADS
DMC six-strand embroidery thread, one skein of each:
Forget-Me-Not Sachet
016 Light Chartreuse
703 Chartreuse
813 Light Blue
800 Blue
740 Tangerine
Queen Anne's Lace Sachet
3608 Plum
153 Lilac
987 Dark Green
470 Light Green

METHOD
Read the instructions for preparing the fabric and marking the centre on page 10. Note that the motif is not placed in the centre of the fabric. Measure 1½in (4cm) up from the bottom edge and baste to mark for the lower edge of the motif. Work the motif, centring it widthwise above the line. Following the chart and colour key, begin stitching at the centre over two fabric threads of the linen fabric using two strands of thread. Stitching area for both sachets: 39 x 45 sts, 2¾ x 3¼in (7 x 8cm).

FINISHING

Remove basting threads. Press lightly from the wrong side on a padded surface. Using small basting stitches, baste 3¼ x 7in (8 x 18cm) centred on the cross-stitched piece. This represents the finished size. Place the cross-stitched piece on top of the unstitched piece of linen fabric with the right sides together. Following the basting lines on the cross-stitched piece, baste the two pieces together on three sides, leaving the top side open. Machine or hand stitch along the basting lines on three sides, leaving the top open. Trim excess any fabric away to ½in (1.3cm) from the seams, except for the top. Trim across the corners. Turn the piece to the right side and square out the corners. Fold in an approx. 1in (2.5cm) hem at the top and sew in place. Using cotton fabric, make a lining bag approx. 3½ x 4½in (9 x 11.5cm). Fill the bag with lavender and sew the top closed. Insert inside the linen embroidery and tie the ribbon in a bow around the top.

FORGET-ME-NOT SACHET

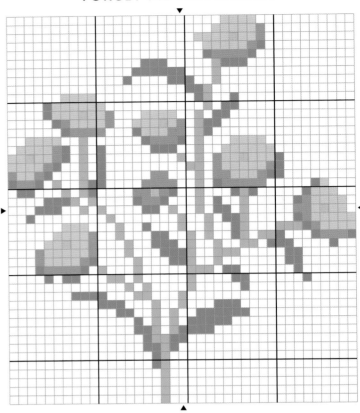

KEY

☐	NO STITCH
▨	016 LIGHT CHARTREUSE
▨	703 CHARTREUSE
▨	813 LIGHT BLUE
▨	800 BLUE
▨	740 TANGERINE

QUEEN ANNE'S LACE SACHET

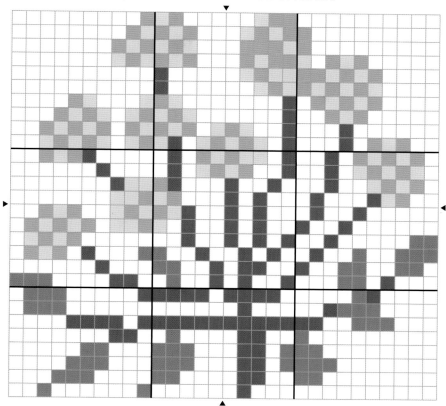

KEY

☐	NO STITCH
▨	3608 PLUM
▨	153 LILAC
■	987 DARK GREEN
▨	470 LIGHT GREEN

NATURE SCENES

SKILL LEVEL: EASY

*These beautiful scenes evoke a love of the great outdoors,
whether hiking in the mountains or relaxing on the beach.*

YOU WILL NEED

MATERIALS
For both
- 11-count white Aida fabric, two pieces measuring 10 x 10in (25 x 25cm)
- Basting thread
- Custom-made frames
- Double-sided tape
- Tapestry needle, no. 24
- Scissors

THREADS
DMC six-strand embroidery thread,
one skein of each:
Seashore
798 Dark Delft Blue
3761 Sky Blue
809 Blue
B5200 Snow White
437 Light Tan
598 Turquoise
807 Peacock Blue

Mountains
B5200 Snow White
001 White Tin
792 Cornflower Blue
340 Medium Violet
341 Light Violet
613 Light Brown
3811 Light Turquoise
800 Pale Blue
501 Blue Green
368 Pistachio Green

METHOD
Read the instructions for preparing the fabric and marking the centre on page 10. Following the chart and colour key, begin stitching at the centre over one square of Aida fabric using three strands of thread.
Stitching area Seashore: 56 x 45 sts, 5 x 4in (12.5 x 10cm)
Stitching area Mountains: 50 x 50 sts, 4¼ x 4¼in (10.5 x 10.5cm)

FINISHING
Remove basting threads. Press lightly from the wrong side on a padded surface. See framing instructions on page 15.

SEASHORE

KEY

☐	NO STITCH
■	798 DARK DELFT BLUE
▨	3761 SKY BLUE
▨	809 BLUE
•	B5200 SNOW WHITE
▨	437 LIGHT TAN
▨	598 TURQUOISE
▨	807 PEACOCK BLUE

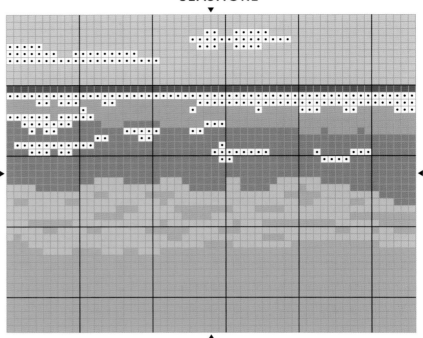

MOUNTAINS

KEY

☐	NO STITCH
•	B5200 SNOW WHITE
╲	001 WHITE TIN
■	792 CORNFLOWER BLUE
▨	340 MEDIUM VIOLET
▨	341 LIGHT VIOLET
▨	613 LIGHT BROWN
▨	3811 LIGHT TURQUOISE
▨	800 PALE BLUE
■	501 BLUE GREEN
▨	368 PISTACHIO GREEN

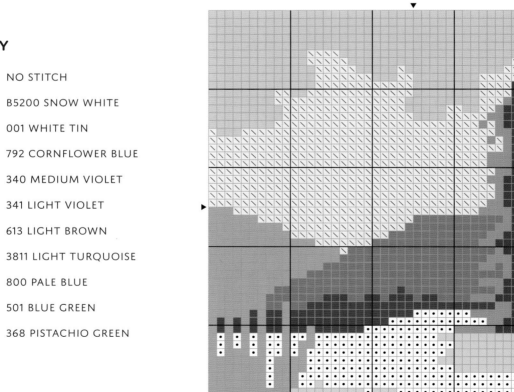

SCALLOP SHELL

FABRIC 14-count white Aida fabric, one piece measuring 8 x 8in (20.5 x 20.5cm)
THREADS DMC six-strand embroidery thread, one skein of each colour listed
HOOP 4in (10cm)
STITCHING AREA 41 x 38 sts, 3 x 2½in (7.5 x 6.5cm)

Read the instructions for preparing the fabric and marking the centre on page 10. Following chart and colour key, begin stitching at the centre over one square of Aida fabric using two strands of thread.

TROPICAL LEAVES

FABRIC 14-count white Aida fabric, one piece measuring 8 x 8in (20.5 x 20.5cm)
THREADS DMC six-strand embroidery thread, one skein of each colour listed
HOOP 4in (10cm)
STITCHING AREA 42 x 45 sts, 3 x 3¼in (7.5 x 8cm)

Read the instructions for preparing the fabric and marking the centre on page 10. Following the chart and colour key, start stitching at the centre over one square of Aida fabric using two strands of thread.

SCALLOP SHELL

KEY

NO STITCH	
023 APPLE BLOSSOM	
025 ULTRA LIGHT LAVENDER	
211 MEDIUM LAVENDER	
209 DARK LAVENDER	

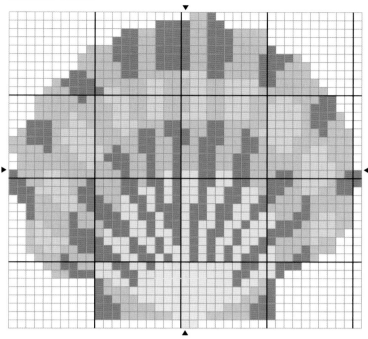

TROPICAL LEAVES

KEY

NO STITCH	
503 MEDIUM BLUE GREEN	
966 MEDIUM BABY GREEN	
988 MEDIUM FOREST GREEN	

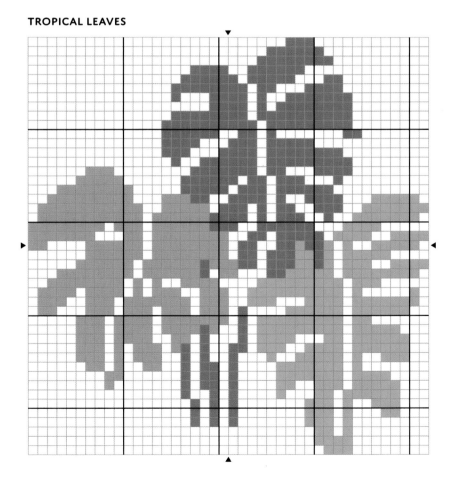

GREEN FEATHER

FABRIC 14-count white Aida fabric, one piece measuring 9 x 9in (23 x 23cm)
THREADS DMC six-strand embroidery thread, one skein of each colour listed
HOOP 5in (12.5cm)
STITCHING AREA 19 x 48 sts, 1¾ x 3½in (4.5 x 9cm)

Read the instructions for preparing the fabric and marking the centre on page 10. Following the chart and colour key, start stitching at the centre over one square of Aida fabric using two strands of thread.

BLUE FEATHER

FABRIC 14-count white Aida fabric, one piece measuring 9 x 9in (23 x 23cm)
THREADS DMC six-strand embroidery thread, one skein of each colour listed
HOOP 5in (12.5cm)
STITCHING AREA 16 x 51 sts, 1¼ x 3¾in (3 x 9.5cm)

Read the instructions for preparing the fabric and marking the centre on page 10. Following the chart and colour key, start stitching at the centre over one square of Aida fabric using two strands of thread.

GREEN FEATHER

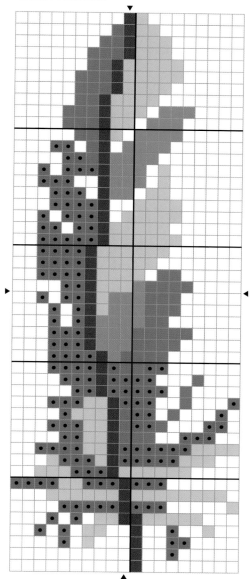

BLUE FEATHER

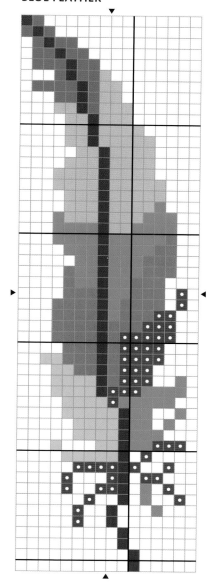

KEY

	NO STITCH
■	702 KELLY GREEN
■•	3850 DARK BRIGHT GREEN
■	958 DARK SEA GREEN
■	598 DARK TURQUOISE
■	3362 DARK PINE GREEN
■	3348 LIGHT YELLOW GREEN

KEY

	NO STITCH
■	702 KELLY GREEN
■	157 LIGHT BLUE
■	799 MEDIUM DELFT BLUE
■•	798 DARK DELFT BLUE
■	958 DARK SEA GREEN
■	3362 DARK PINE GREEN
■	598 LIGHT TURQUOISE

NAUTILUS SHELL

FABRIC 14-count pale blue Aida fabric, one piece measuring 8 x 8in (20.5 x 20.5cm)
THREADS DMC six-strand embroidery thread, one skein of each colour listed
HOOP 4in (10cm)
STITCHING AREA 51 x 37 sts, 3½ x 2in (9 x 5cm)

Read the instructions for preparing the fabric and marking the centre on page 10. Following the chart and colour key, start stitching at the centre over one square of Aida fabric using two strands of thread.

CRESTING WAVE

FABRIC 14-count pale blue Aida fabric, one piece measuring 8 x 8in (20.5 x 20.5cm)
THREADS DMC six-strand embroidery thread, one skein of each colour listed
HOOP 4in (10cm)
STITCHING AREA 50 x 46 sts, 3½ x 3¼in (9 x 8cm)

Read the instructions for preparing the fabric and marking the centre on page 10. Following the chart and colour key, start stitching at the centre over one square of Aida fabric using two strands of thread.

NAUTILUS SHELL

KEY

☐ NO STITCH

■ 3778 LIGHT TERRA COTTA

■ 3771 DARK PEACH

■ 3774 VERY LIGHT DESERT SAND

● 778 VERY LIGHT ANTIQUE MAUVE

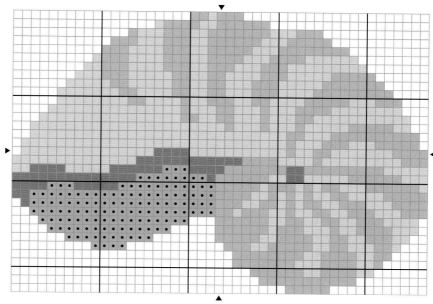

CRESTING WAVE

KEY

☐ NO STITCH

● B5200 SNOW WHITE

■ 437 LIGHT TAN

■ 959 MEDIUM SEA GREEN

■ 943 MEDIUM AQUAMARINE

■ 3760 WEDGEWOOD

■ 3841 PALE BABY BLUE

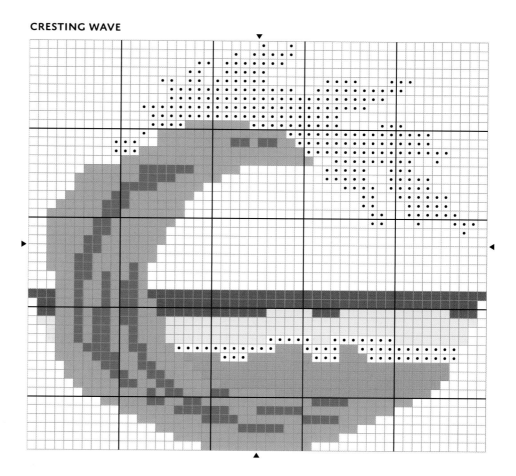

TINY TOADSTOOL

FABRIC 14-count white Aida fabric, one piece measuring 8 x 8in (20.5 x 20.5cm)
THREADS DMC six-strand embroidery thread, one skein of each colour listed
HOOP 4in (10cm)
STITCHING AREA 32 x 45 sts, 2¼ x 3¼in (5.5 x 8cm)

Read the instructions for preparing the fabric and marking the centre on page 10. Following the chart and colour key, start stitching at the centre over one square of Aida fabric using two strands of thread. Work backstitches using one strand of 009 thread.

FOREST MUSHROOMS

FABRIC 14-count white Aida fabric, one piece measuring 8 x 8in (20.5 x 20.5cm)
THREADS DMC six-strand embroidery thread, one skein of each colour listed
HOOP 4in (10cm)
STITCHING AREA 35 x 37 sts, 2¼ x 2½in (5.5 x 6.5cm)

Read the instructions for preparing the fabric and marking the centre on page 10. Following the chart and colour key, start stitching at the centre over one square of Aida fabric using two strands of thread. Work backstitches using one strand of 009 thread.

TINY TOADSTOOL

KEY

- NO STITCH
- 987 DARK FOREST GREEN
- 703 CHARTREUSE
- 922 LIGHT COPPER
- 402 VERY LIGHT MAHOGANY
- 019 MEDIUM LIGHT AUTUMN GOLD
- 842 VERY LIGHT BEIGE BROWN
- 008 DARK DRIFTWOOD
- 407 DARK DESERT SAND
- 009 VERY DARK COCOA

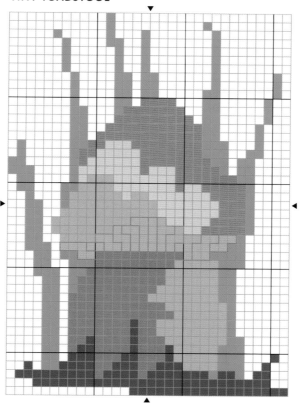

FOREST MUSHROOMS

KEY

- NO STITCH
- 005 LIGHT DRIFTWOOD
- ~ 842 BEIGE BROWN
- 841 VERY LIGHT BEIGE BROWN
- 817 VERY DARK CORAL RED
- 608 BRIGHTORANGE
- 905 DARK PARROT GREEN
- 703 CHARTREUSE
- 009 VERY DARK COCOA

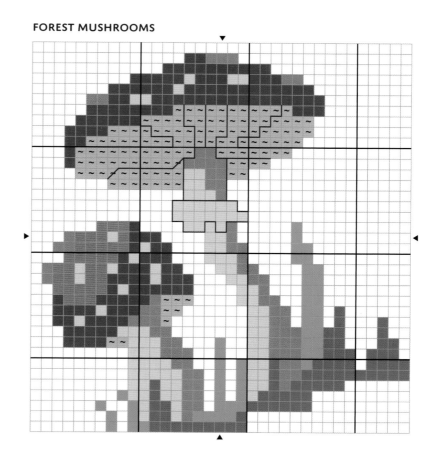

PRICKLY PEAR

FABRIC 14-count white fabric, one piece measuring 9 x 9in (23 x 23cm)
THREADS DMC six-strand embroidery thread, one skein of each colour listed
HOOP 5in (12.5cm)
STITCHING AREA 31 x 59 sts, 2¼ x 4¼in (5.5 x 10.5cm)

Read the instructions for preparing the fabric and marking the centre on page 10. Following the chart and colour key, start stitching at the centre over one square of Aida fabric using two strands of thread. Work backstitches using one strand of 310 thread.

FLOWERING CACTUS

FABRIC 14-count white Aida fabric, one piece measuring 8 x 8in (20.5 x 20.5cm)
THREADS DMC six-strand embroidery thread, one skein of each colour listed
HOOP 4in (10cm)
STITCHING AREA 41 x 34 sts, 3 x 2½in (7.5 x 6.5cm)

Read the instructions for preparing the fabric and marking the centre on page 10. Following the chart and colour key, start stitching at the centre over one square of Aida fabric using two strands of thread. Work backstitches using one strand of 3607 and 501 thread.

PRICKLY PEAR

FLOWERING CACTUS

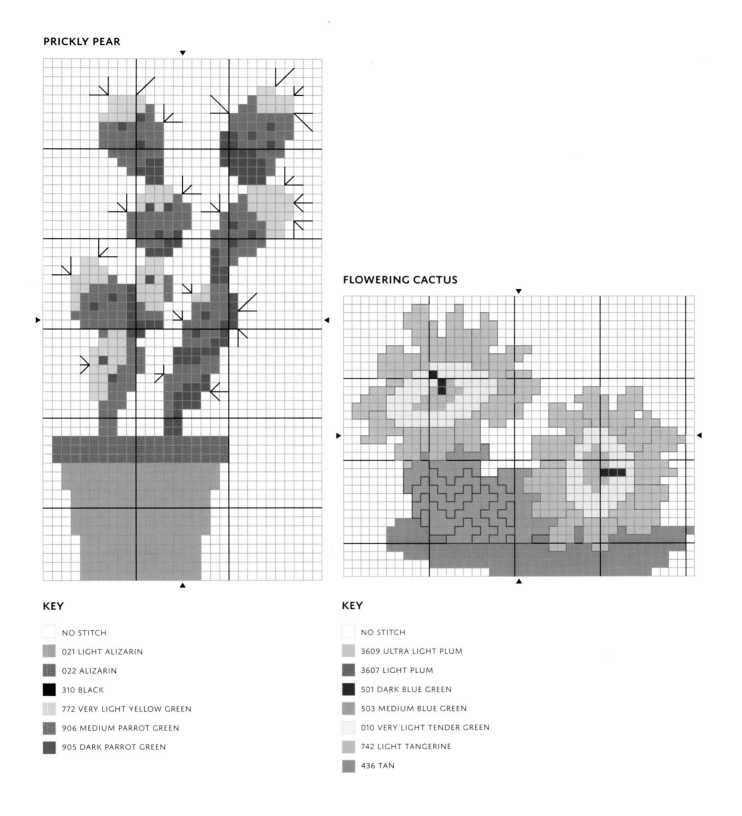

KEY

- NO STITCH
- 021 LIGHT ALIZARIN
- 022 ALIZARIN
- 310 BLACK
- 772 VERY LIGHT YELLOW GREEN
- 906 MEDIUM PARROT GREEN
- 905 DARK PARROT GREEN

KEY

- NO STITCH
- 3609 ULTRA LIGHT PLUM
- 3607 LIGHT PLUM
- 501 DARK BLUE GREEN
- 503 MEDIUM BLUE GREEN
- 010 VERY LIGHT TENDER GREEN
- 742 LIGHT TANGERINE
- 436 TAN

GEODE SLICE

FABRIC 14-count white Aida fabric, one piece measuring 9 x 9in (23 x 23cm)
THREADS DMC six-strand embroidery thread, one skein of each colour listed
HOOP 5in (12.5cm)
STITCHING AREA 52 x 33 sts, 3¾ x 2¼in (9.5 x 5.5cm)

Read the instructions for preparing the fabric and marking the centre on page 10. Following the chart and colour key, begin stitching at the centre over one square of Aida fabric using two strands of thread. Work backstitches using one strand of 958 thread.

AMETHYST CRYSTAL

FABRIC 14-count white Aida fabric, one piece measuring 8 x 8in (20.5 x 20.5cm)
THREADS DMC six-strand embroidery thread, one skein of each colour listed
HOOP 4in (10cm)
STITCHING AREA 38 x 49 sts, 2¾ x 3½in (7 x 9cm)

Read the instructions for preparing the fabric and marking the centre on page 10. Following the chart and colour key, start stitching at the centre over one square of Aida fabric using two strands of thread.

GEODE SLICE

KEY

NO STITCH
747 VERY LIGHT SKY BLUE
958 DARK SEA GREEN
964 LIGHT SEA GREEN
702 KELLY GREEN
742 LIGHT TANGERINE

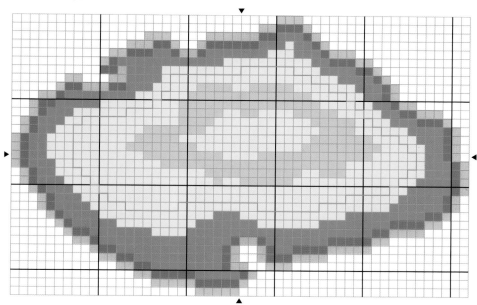

AMETHYST CRYSTAL

KEY

NO STITCH
800 PALE DELFT BLUE
826 MEDIUM BLUE
813 LIGHT BLUE
825 DARK BLUE
327 VIOLET
211 LIGHT LAVENDER
210 MEDIUM LAVENDER
209 DARK LAVENDER

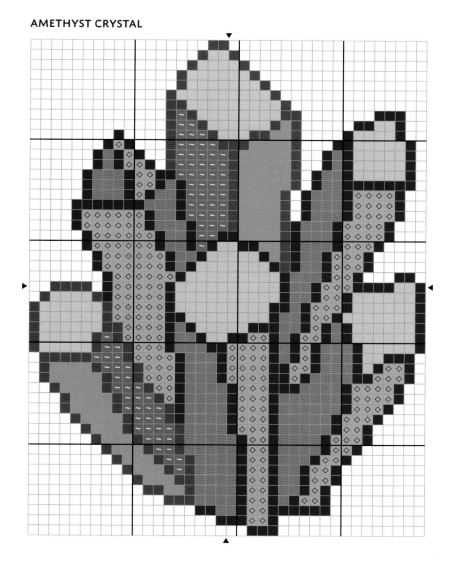

PINK DAISY

FABRIC 14-count white Aida fabric, one piece measuring 8 x 8in (20.5 x 20.5cm)
THREADS DMC six-strand embroidery thread, one skein of each colour listed
HOOP 4in (10cm)
STITCHING AREA 43 x 43 sts, 3 x 3in (7.5 x 7.5cm)

Read the instructions for preparing the fabric and marking the centre on page 10. Following the chart and colour key, start stitching at the centre over one square of Aida fabric using two strands of thread.

RAMBLING LEAVES

FABRIC 14-count white Aida fabric, one piece measuring 9 x 9in (23 x 23cm)
THREADS DMC six-strand embroidery thread, one skein of each colour listed
HOOP 5in (12.5cm)
STITCHING AREA 57 x 57 sts, 4 x 4in (10 x 10cm)

Read the instructions for preparing the fabric and marking the centre on page 10. Following the chart and colour key, start stitching at the centre over one square of Aida fabric using two strands of thread. Work backstitches using one strand of 988 thread.

PINK DAISY

KEY

☐ NO STITCH

■ 963 ULTRA VERY LIGHT DUSTY ROSE

■ 605 VERY LIGHT CRANBERRY

■ 3806 LIGHT CYCLAMEN PINK

■ 368 LIGHT PISTACHIO GREEN

■ 369 VERY LIGHT PISTACHIO GREEN

• B5200 SNOW WHITE

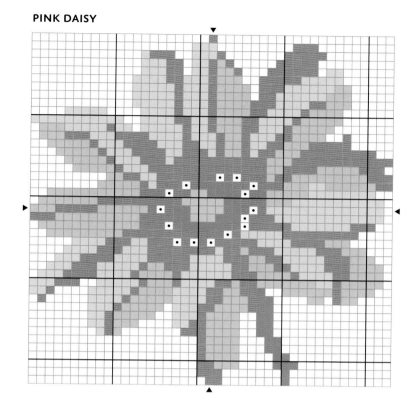

RAMBLING LEAVES

KEY

☐ NO STITCH

■ 966 MEDIUM BABY GREEN

■ 3013 LIGHT KHAKI GREEN

■ 988 MEDIUM FOREST GREEN

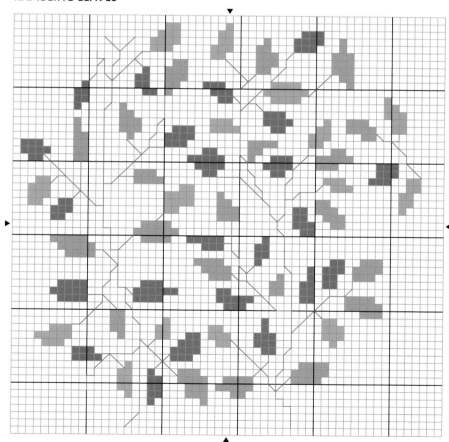

POTTED CROCUS

FABRIC 14-count white Aida fabric, one piece measuring 8 x 8in (20.5 x 20.5cm)
THREADS DMC six-strand embroidery thread, one skein of each colour listed
HOOP 4in (10cm)
STITCHING AREA 33 x 38 sts, 2¼ x 2¾in (5.5 x 7cm)

Read the instructions for preparing the fabric and marking the centre on page 10. Following the chart and colour key, start stitching at the centre over one square of Aida fabric using two strands of thread. Work backstitches using one strand of 936 thread.

POTTED CROCUS

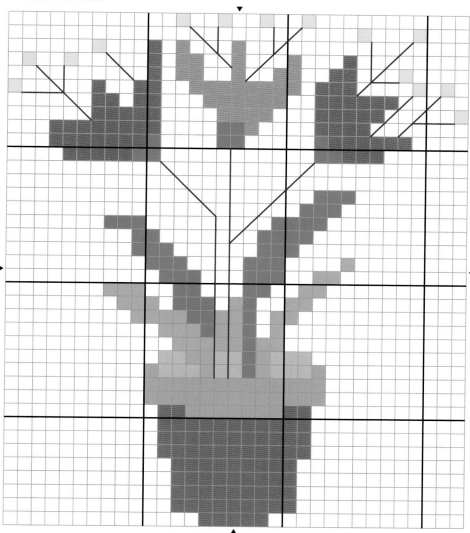

KEY

	NO STITCH
	021 LIGHT ALIZARIN
	022 ALIZARIN
	704 BRIGHT CHARTREUSE
	702 KELLY GREEN
	033 FUCHSIA
	3608 VERY LIGHT PLUM
	743 MEDIUM YELLOW
	936 VERY DARK AVOCADO GREEN
	007 DRIFTWOOD

ICE POP TRIPTYCH

SKILL LEVEL: EASY

*These three framed ice pops in light pastel colours will
add a whimsical touch to any room.*

YOU WILL NEED

MATERIALS
For each ice pop
- 14-count white Aida fabric, one piece measuring 5 x 6in (12.5 x 15cm)
- Basting thread
- One 3 x 4in (7.5 x 10cm) frame
- Tapestry needle, no. 24
- Scissors
- Double-sided tape

THREADS
DMC six-strand embroidery thread,
one skein of each:
Blueberry Ice Pop
813 Light Blue
800 Pale Delft Blue
437 Light Tan
Lemon Ice Pop
972 Deep Canary
743 Medium Yellow
437 Light Tan
B5200 Snow White

Berry Ice Pop
033 Fuchsia
3806 Light Cyclamen Pink
151 Pink
3836 Light Grape
437 Light Tan

METHOD
Read the instructions for preparing the fabric and marking the centre on page 10. Following the chart and colour key, begin stitching at the centre over one square of Aida fabric using two strands of thread.

FINISHING
Press lightly from the wrong side on a padded surface. See framing instructions on page 15.

TIP
Cut thread to the distance between your hand and your elbow to reduce the risk of knots.

BLUEBERRY ICE POP

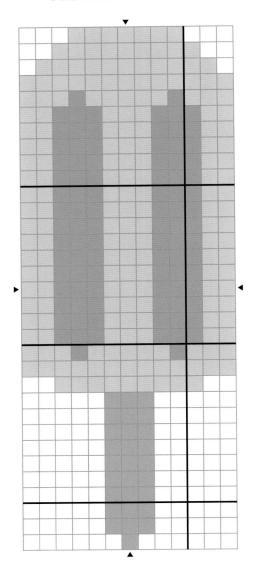

LEMON ICE POP

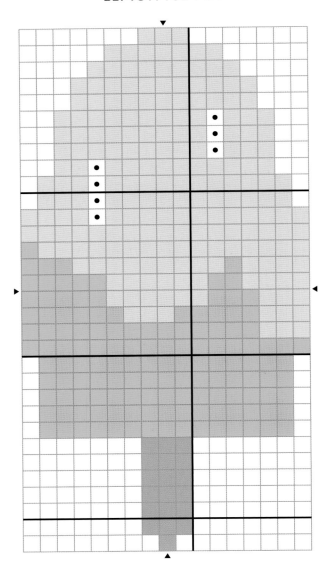

KEY

	NO STITCH
	813 LIGHT BLUE
	800 PALE DELFT BLUE
	437 LIGHT TAN

KEY

	NO STITCH
	972 DEEP CANARY
	743 MEDIUM YELLOW
	437 LIGHT TAN
•	B5200 SNOW WHITE

BERRY ICE POP

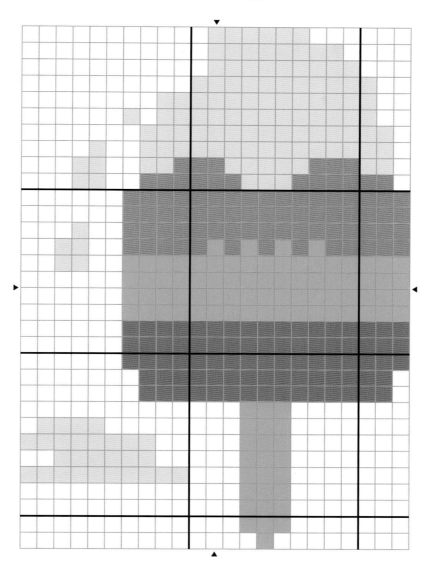

KEY

	NO STITCH
	033 FUCHSIA
	3806 LIGHT CYCLAMEN PINK
	151 PINK
	3836 LIGHT GRAPE
	437 LIGHT TAN

BIRTHDAY CARDS

SKILL LEVEL: EASY

Towering buttercream frosting on chocolate and blueberry cupcakes, and strawberry ice cream in a waffle cone are too tempting not to stitch!

YOU WILL NEED

MATERIALS
For each card
- 11-count white Aida fabric, one piece measuring 5½ x 7in (14 x 18cm)
- Basting thread
- Frame card 5 x 7in (12.5 x 18cm) with oval opening 3½ x 5in (9 x 12.5cm)
- Tapestry needle, no. 24
- Scissors
- Double-sided tape

THREADS
DMC six-strand embroidery thread, one skein of each:

Blueberry Cupcake
3805 Cyclamen Pink
606 Bright Orange Red
975 Dark Golden Brown
794 Light Cornflower Blue
407 Dark Desert Sand
151 Pink
950 Light Desert Sand
311 Medium Blue
B5200 Snow White

Chocolate Cupcake
963 Ultra Very Light Dusty Rose
945 Tawny
975 Dark Golden Brown
407 Dark Desert Sand
151 Pink
3805 Cyclamen Pink

Ice Cream Cone
950 Light Desert Sand
3722 Very Dark Desert Sand
151 Pink
3806 Light Cyclamen Pink

TIP
For an extra treat, include a recipe for their favourite cupcake inside the card.

METHOD

Read the instructions for preparing the fabric and marking the centre on page 10. Following the chart and colour key, begin stitching at the centre over one square of Aida fabric using three strands of thread.

Stitching area Ice Cream Cone
19 x 39 sts, 1¾ x 3½in (4.5 x 9cm)
Stitching area Blueberry Cupcake
30 x 35 sts, 2¾ x 3in (7 x 7.5cm)
Stitching area Chocolate Cupcake
26 x 38 sts, 2½ x 3½in (6.5 x 9cm)

Work backstitches on Blueberry Cupcake using two strands of 3805 thread.

FINISHING

Press lightly from the wrong side on a padded surface. Mark from the centre 2½in (6.5cm) each side horizontally and 3½in (9cm) vertically (for a rectangle 5 x 7in [12.5 x 18cm]). Trim the excess fabric and remove centre basting threads. Apply double-sided tape to the inside of the card. Centre the finished piece in the card window, then press to adhere to the tape.

BLUEBERRY CUPCAKE

KEY

☐ NO STITCH

■ 3805 CYCLAMEN PINK

■ 606 BRIGHT ORANGE RED

■ 975 DARK GOLDEN BROWN

■ 794 LIGHT CORNFLOWER BLUE

■ 407 DARK DESERT SAND

■ 151 PINK

■ 950 LIGHT DESERT SAND

■ 311 MEDIUM BLUE

• B5200 SNOW WHITE

CHOCOLATE CUPCAKE

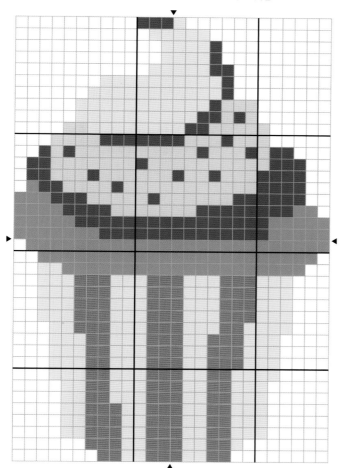

ICE CREAM CONE

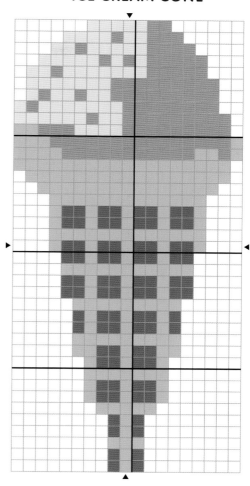

KEY

	NO STITCH
■	963 ULTRA VERY LIGHT DUSTY ROSE
■	945 TAWNY
■	975 DARK GOLDEN BROWN
■	407 DARK DESERT SAND
■	151 PINK
■	3805 CYCLAMEN PINK

KEY

	NO STITCH
■	950 LIGHT DESERT SAND
■	3722 VERY DARK DESERT SAND
■	151 PINK
■	3806 LIGHT CYCLAMEN PINK

WINE GLASS NAPKIN

SKILL LEVEL: EASY

Purchasing a small towel with an Aida band inset makes it simple to create a useful gift that is quick and easy to cross stitch.

YOU WILL NEED

MATERIALS
- Tea towel or hand towel measuring 12 x 19.5in (30.5 x 49.5cm) with 14-count Aida inset
- Basting thread
- Tapestry needle, no. 24
- Scissors

THREADS
DMC six-strand embroidery thread, one skein of each:
712 Cream
309 Dark Rose
816 Garnet
415 Pearl Grey
001 White Tin
B5200 Snow White

METHOD
Read the instructions for preparing the fabric and marking the centre on **page 10**, and baste the Aida band. Following the chart and colour key, begin stitching at the centre over one square of the Aida band using two strands of thread. Stitching area: 45 x 27 sts, 3¼ x 2in (8.5 x 5cm).

FINISHING
Remove basting threads. Press lightly from the wrong side on a padded surface.

TIP
When stitching onto the towel, keep your stitches as neat as possible, as both sides will be visible.

WINE GLASS NAPKIN

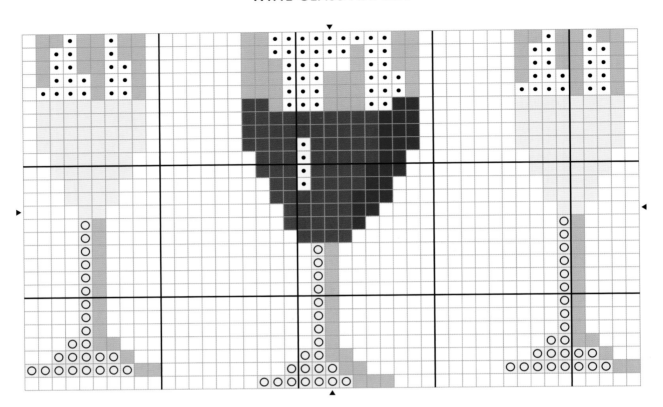

KEY

☐ NO STITCH

☐ 712 CREAM

■ 309 DARK ROSE

■ 816 GARNET

■ 415 PEARL GREY

○ 001 WHITE TIN

• B5200 SNOW WHITE

BLOODY MARY

FABRIC 14-count white Aida fabric, one piece measuring 8 x 8in (20.5 x 20.5cm)
THREADS DMC six-strand embroidery thread, one skein of each colour listed
HOOP 4in (10cm)
STITCHING AREA 22 x 49 sts, 1½ x 3½in (4 x 9cm)

Read the instructions for preparing the fabric and marking the centre on page 10. Following the chart and colour key, start stitching at the centre over one square of Aida fabric using two strands of thread. Work backstitches using two strands of 840 thread for the olive toothpick and one strand of 004 thread for the outline.

SUMMER COCKTAIL

FABRIC 14-count white Aida fabric, one piece measuring 8 x 8in (20.5 x 20.5cm)
THREADS DMC six-strand embroidery thread, one skein of each colour listed
HOOP 4in (10cm)
STITCHING AREA 33 x 51 sts, 2¼ x 3½in (5.5 x 9cm)

Read the instructions for preparing the fabric and marking the centre on page 10. Following the chart and colour key, start stitching at the centre over one square of Aida fabric using two strands of thread. Work backstitches using one strand of 900 thread.

BLOODY MARY

SUMMER COCKTAIL

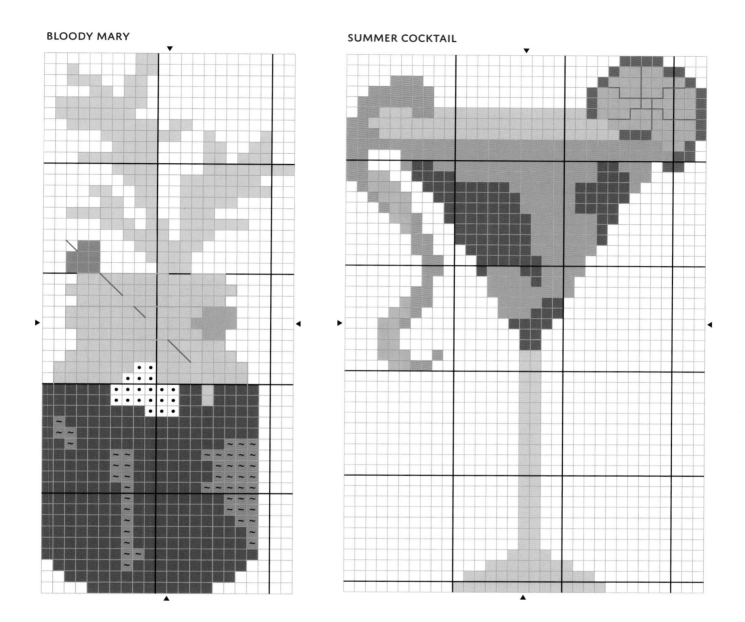

KEY

	NO STITCH
	004 DARK TIN
	472 ULTRA LIGHT AVOCADO GREEN
•	B5200 SNOW WHITE
	3347 MEDIUM YELLOW GREEN
	002 TIN
	817 VERY DARK CORAL RED
~	3712 MEDIUM SALMON
	840 MEDIUM BEIGE BROWN

KEY

	NO STITCH
	741 MEDIUM TANGERINE
	970 LIGHT PUMPKIN
	900 DARK BURNT ORANGE
	001 WHITE TIN
	309 DARK ROSE
	3688 MEDIUM MAUVE

MAKI SUSHI

FABRIC 14-count white Aida fabric, one piece measuring 8 x 8in (20.5 x 20.5cm)
THREADS DMC six-strand embroidery thread, one skein of each colour listed
HOOP 4in (10cm)
STITCHING AREA 40 x 19 sts, 2¾ x 1¼in (7 x 4.5cm)

Read the instructions for preparing the fabric and marking the centre on page 10. Following the chart and colour key, start stitching at the centre over one square of Aida fabric using two strands of thread. Work backstitches using one strand of 310 thread.

MAKI SUSHI AND CHOPSTICKS

FABRIC 14-count white Aida fabric, one piece measuring 8 x 8in (20.5 x 20.5cm)
THREADS DMC six-strand embroidery thread, one skein of each colour listed
HOOP 4in (10cm)
STITCHING AREA 46 x 22 sts, 3¼ x 1½in (8 x 4cm)

Read the instructions for preparing the fabric and marking the centre on page 10. Following the chart and colour key, start stitching at the centre over one square of Aida fabric using two strands of thread.

MAKI SUSHI

KEY

☐ NO STITCH
• B5200 SNOW WHITE
■ 900 BURNT ORANGE - DK
■ 3348 LIGHT YELLOW GREEN
■ 310 BLACK
■ 738 VERY LIGHT TAN
■ 3347 MEDIUM YELLOW GREEN

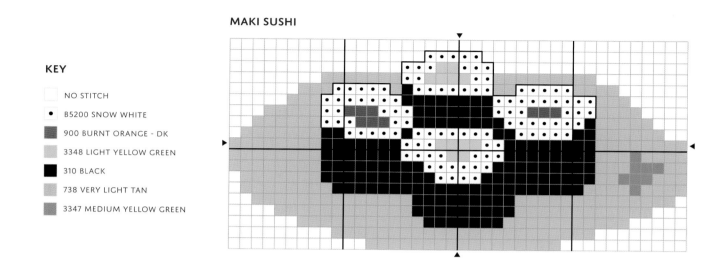

MAKI SUSHI AND CHOPSTICKS

KEY

☐ NO STITCH
• B5200 SNOW WHITE
■ 310 BLACK
■ 505 DARK GREEN
■ 900 DARK BURNT ORANGE
■ 738 VERY LIGHT TAN
■ 437 LIGHT TAN
■ 3347 MEDIUM YELLOW GREEN

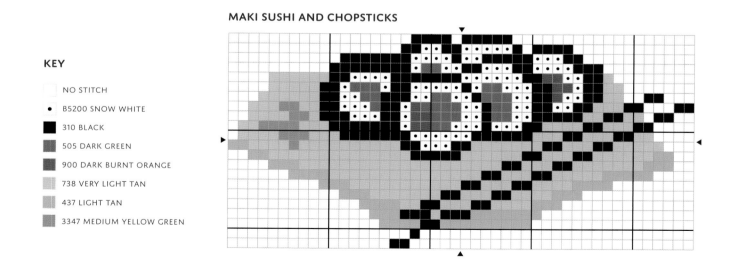

WATERMELON

FABRIC 14-count white Aida fabric, one piece measuring 7 x 7in (18 x 18cm)
THREADS DMC six-strand embroidery thread, one skein of each colour listed
HOOP 3in (7.5cm)
STITCHING AREA 33 x 28 sts, 2¼ x 2in (5.5 x 5cm)

Read the instructions for preparing the fabric and marking the centre on page 10. Following the chart and colour key, start stitching at the centre over one square of Aida fabric using two strands of thread. Work backstitches using one strand of 910 thread.

MACARONS

FABRIC 14-count white Aida fabric, one piece measuring 8 x 8in (20.5 x 20.5cm)
THREADS DMC six-strand embroidery thread, one skein of each colour listed
HOOP 4in (10cm)
STITCHING AREA 33 x 36 sts, 2½ x 2½in (6.5 x 6.5cm)

Read the instructions for preparing the fabric and marking the centre on page 10. Following the chart and colour key, start stitching at the centre over one square of Aida fabric using two strands of thread. Work backstitches using one strand of 799 thread.

WATERMELON

KEY

☐	NO STITCH
■	310 BLACK
	3805 CYCLAMEN PINK
	3608 VERY LIGHT PLUM
	910 DARK EMERALD GREEN
	013 MEDIUM LIGHT NILE GREEN
	015 APPLE GREEN

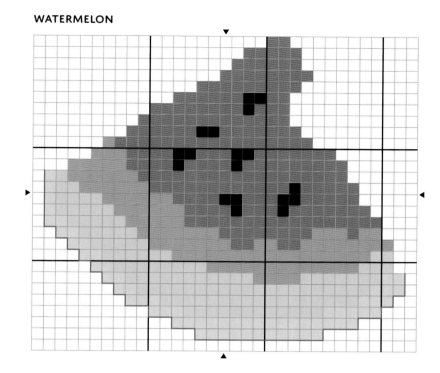

MACARONS

KEY

☐	NO STITCH
	3687 MAUVE
	603 CRANBERRY
	3609 ULTRA LIGHT PLUM
	032 DARK BLUEBERRY
	030 MEDIUM LIGHT BLUEBERRY
	026 PALE LAVENDER
	912 LIGHT EMERALD GREEN
	015 APPLE GREEN
	013 MEDIUM LIGHT NILE GREEN
	799 MEDIUM DELFT BLUE
•	B5200 SNOW WHITE

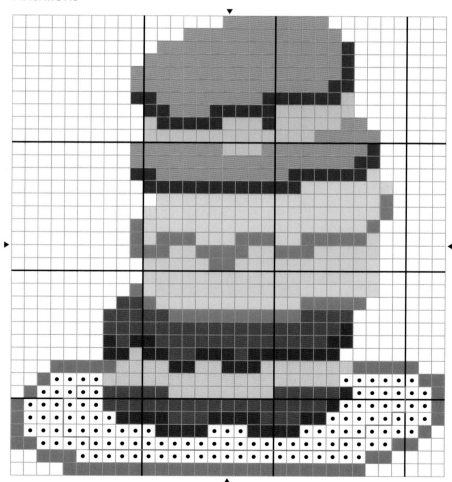

BIRTHDAY CAKE

FABRIC 14-count white Aida fabric, one piece measuring 8 x 8in (20.5 x 20.5cm)
THREADS DMC six-strand embroidery thread, one skein of each colour listed
HOOP 4in (10cm)
STITCHING AREA 39 x 37 sts, 2¾ x 2¾in (7 x 7cm)

Read the instructions for preparing the fabric and marking the centre on page 10. Following the chart and colour key, start stitching at the centre over one square of Aida fabric using two strands of thread. Work backstitches using one strand of 151 thread.

EGG IN A CUP

FABRIC 14-count white Aida fabric, one piece measuring 8 x 8in (20.5 x 20.5cm)
THREADS DMC six-strand embroidery thread, one skein of each colour listed
HOOP 4in (10cm)
STITCHING AREA 29 x 43 sts, 2 x 3in (5 x 7.5cm)

Read the instructions for preparing the fabric and marking the centre on page 10. Following the chart and colour key, start stitching at the centre over one square of Aida fabric using two strands of thread. Work backstitches using one strand of 004 thread.

BIRTHDAY CAKE

KEY

	NO STITCH
■	407 DARK DESERT SAND
■	437 LIGHT TAN
■	151 PINK
■	3833 LIGHT RASPBERRY
■	309 DARK ROSE
■	813 LIGHT BLUE
•	B5200 SNOW WHITE
■	742 LIGHT TANGERINE

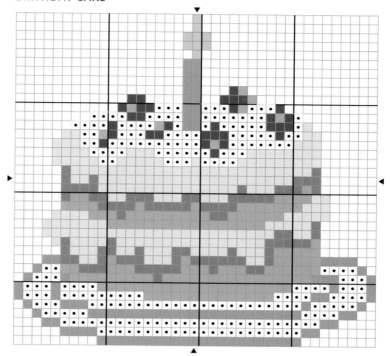

EGG IN A CUP

KEY

	NO STITCH
■	3771 DARK PEACH
■	3778 LIGHT TERRA COTTA
■	003 MEDIUM TIN
■	004 DARK TIN
■	3849 LIGHT TEAL GREEN
•	B5200 SNOW WHITE
■	741 MEDIUM TANGERINE

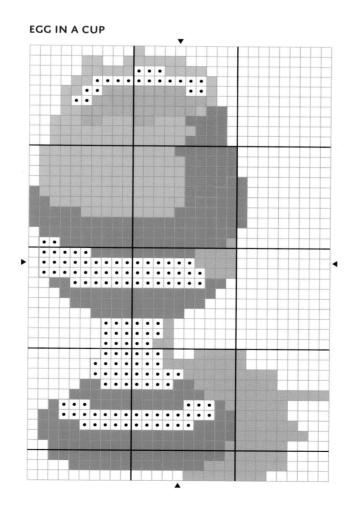

FRAMED DINOSAURS

SKILL LEVEL: EASY

These delightful dinosaurs, framed as a group or individually, will be loved by little kids and make a lovely addition to their room.

YOU WILL NEED

MATERIALS
- 14-count white Aida fabric, one piece measuring 6 x 8in (15 x 20.5cm)
- Basting thread
- One frame 9¾ x 16½in (25 x 42cm) with three 4 x 6in (10 x 15cm) openings
- Tapestry needle, no. 24
- Scissors
- Double-sided tape

THREADS
DMC six-strand embroidery thread, one skein of each:

Brontosaurus
958 Dark Green
310 Black
3746 Dark Violet

Stegosaurus
666 Bright Red
310 Black
970 Light Pumpkin

T-Rex
703 Chartreuse
310 Black

METHOD
Read the instructions for preparing the fabric and marking the centre on page 10. Following the chart and colour key, begin stitching at the centre over one square of Aida fabric using two strands of thread.
Stitching area Brontosaurus: 28 x 37 sts, 2 x 2½in (5 x 6.5cm)
Stitching area Stegosaurus: 36 x 21 sts, 2½ x 1½in (6.5 x 4cm)
Stitching area T-Rex: 44 x 37 sts, 3¼ x 2½in (8 x 6.5cm)

FINISHING
Press lightly on the wrong side on a padded surface. See framing instructions on page 15.

TIP
These cute dinosaurs would also look great on children's clothing, walking across the edge of a bed pillow, or on a pencil case.

BRONTOSAURUS

KEY

☐	NO STITCH
■	958 DARK GREEN
■	310 BLACK
■	3746 DARK VIOLET

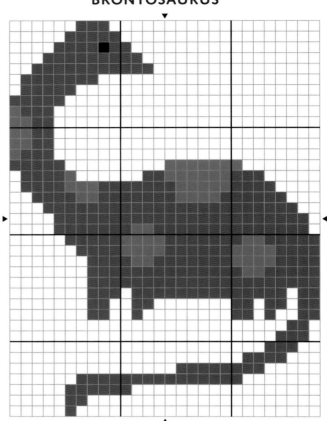

STEGOSAURUS

KEY

☐	NO STITCH
•	606 BRIGHT RED
■	310 BLACK
■	970 LIGHT PUMPKIN

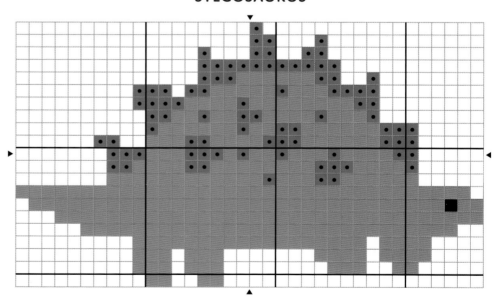

T-REX

KEY

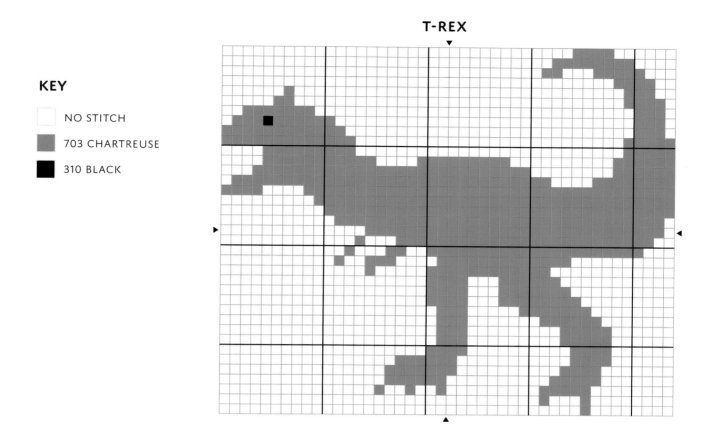

☐ NO STITCH

▨ 703 CHARTREUSE

■ 310 BLACK

FRAMED ROCKETS

SKILL LEVEL: EASY

*This adorable trio of rockets, showing the countdown, blast-off and orbit,
is the perfect wall art for a budding astronaut.*

YOU WILL NEED

MATERIALS
For each rocket
- 14-count white Aida fabric, one piece measuring 12 x 12in (30.5 x 30.5cm)
- Basting thread
- Three frames each 8½ x 8½in (21.5 x 21.5cm) with 4½ x 4½in (11.5 x 11.5cm) opening
- Tapestry needle, no. 24
- Scissors
- Double-sided tape

THREADS
DMC six-strand embroidery thread,
one skein of each:
Countdown
666 Bright Red
725 Topaz
3845 Bright Turquoise
798 Dark Delft Blue
Blast Off
666 Bright Red
725 Topaz
762 Light Grey
798 Dark Delft Blue

Orbiting
666 Bright Red
310 Black
725 Topaz
798 Dark Delft Blue
3845 Bright Turquoise

METHOD
Read the instructions for preparing the fabric and marking the centre on page 10. Following the chart and colour key, begin stitching at the centre over one square of Aida fabric using two strands of thread. For Orbiting: Work backstitches using two strands of 310 thread.

Stitching area Countdown: 27 x 55 sts, 1¾ x 4in (4.5 x 10cm)
Stitching area Blast Off: 21 x 50 sts, 1½ x 3½in (4 x 9cm)
Stitching area Orbiting: 33 x 39 sts, 2¼ x 2¾in (6.5 x 7cm)

FINISHING
Press lightly on the wrong side on a padded surface. See framing instructions on page 15.

COUNTDOWN

BLAST OFF

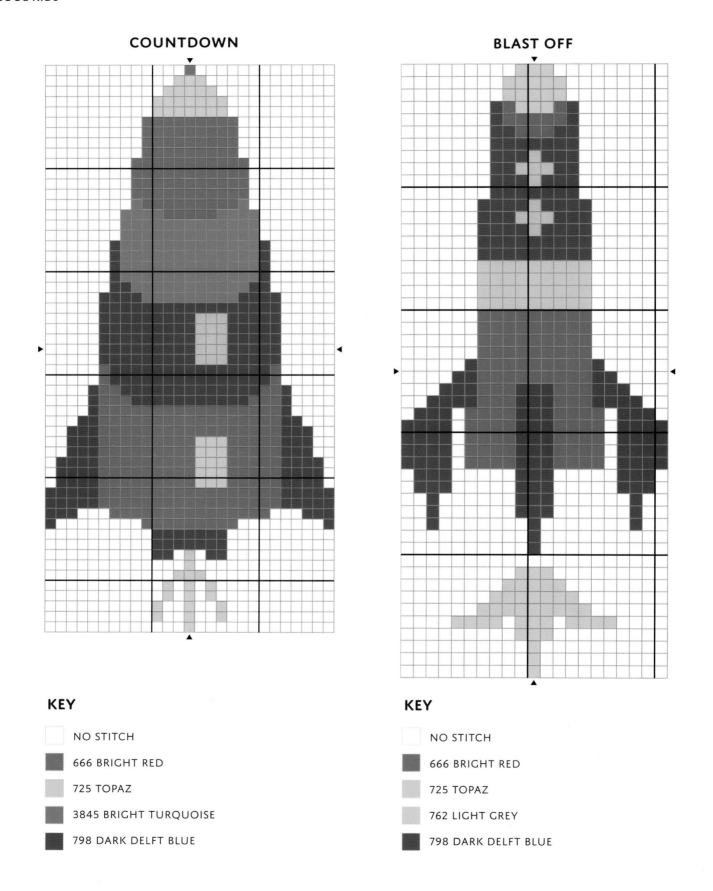

KEY

	NO STITCH
	666 BRIGHT RED
	725 TOPAZ
	3845 BRIGHT TURQUOISE
	798 DARK DELFT BLUE

KEY

	NO STITCH
	666 BRIGHT RED
	725 TOPAZ
	762 LIGHT GREY
	798 DARK DELFT BLUE

ORBITING

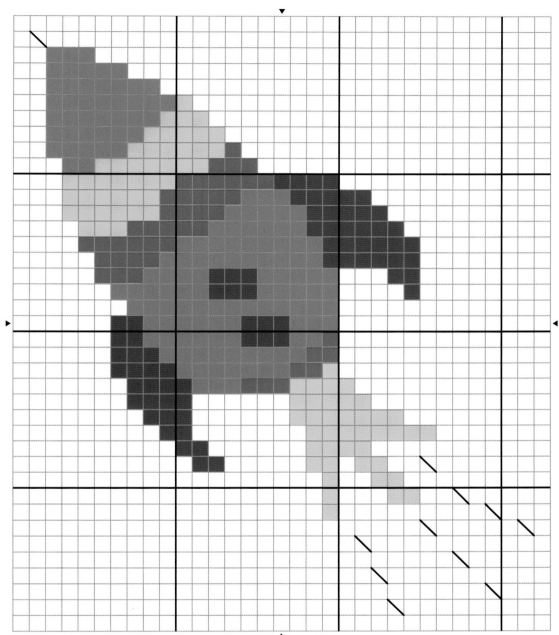

KEY

	NO STITCH
▪	666 BRIGHT RED
■	310 BLACK
▪	725 TOPAZ
▪	798 DARK DELFT BLUE
▪	3845 BRIGHT TURQUOISE

TRAIN PILLOW

SKILL LEVEL: INTERMEDIATE

Young railway enthusiasts will love this colourful steam train, and a few finishing touches will turn your work into something they can keep forever.

YOU WILL NEED

MATERIALS
- 11-count white Aida fabric, one piece measuring 16 x 12in (40.5 x 30.5cm)
- Blue cotton fabric 16 x 12in (40.5 x 30.5cm) for pillow backing
- Fibrefill for stuffing
- Basting thread
- Tapestry needle, no. 24
- Sewing needle and thread or sewing machine
- Scissors

THREADS
DMC six-strand embroidery thread, one skein of each:
310 Black
817 Dark Red
796 Dark Blue
958 Dark Green
742 Tangerine
B5200 Snow White

METHOD
Read the instructions for preparing the fabric and marking the centre on page 10. Following the chart and colour key, begin stitching at the centre over one square of Aida fabric using three strands of thread. Stitching area: 95 x 18 sts, 8½ x 1½in (22 x 4cm).

FINISHING
Press lightly on the wrong side on a padded surface. Baste a 8 x 12in (20 x 30.5cm) rectangle (this will be the finished size of the pillow) around the stitched area, with the motif centred. Place the cotton backing fabric over the cross-stitched piece with right sides together. Following the basting line on the Aida fabric, baste the pillow back and cross-stitched pieces together. Machine stitch, or use tiny backstitches to hand sew, around three sides (one shorter and two longer sides), and 1in (2.5cm) in from each end on the fourth side. Remove basting thread, trim away the excess fabric to ½in (1.3cm) from the seams. Trim across the corners. Turn to the right side, square out the corners and press. Fill with fibrefill to the desired firmness. Hand-sew the fourth side closed.

TRAIN PILLOW

KEY

☐	NO STITCH
■	310 BLACK
■	817 DARK RED
■	796 DARK BLUE
■	958 DARK GREEN
☐	740 TANGERINE
•	B5200 SNOW WHITE

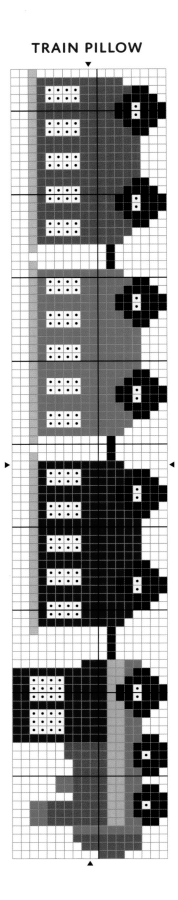

BALLOON CARD

SKILL LEVEL: EASY

*Cards with windows, usually intended for holding photos,
are a perfect way to showcase cross stitch.*

YOU WILL NEED

MATERIALS
- 14-count white Aida fabric, one piece measuring 5½ x 7in (14 x 18 cm)
- Frame card 5 x 7in (12.7 x 17.7cm) with opening 3½in x 5½in (9 x 14cm)
- Basting thread
- Double-sided tape
- Tapestry needle, no. 24
- Scissors

THREADS
DMC six-strand embroidery thread,
one skein of each:
3837 Dark Lavender
740 Tangerine
742 Light Tangerine
703 Chartreuse
3845 Medium Turquoise
964 Medium Orange
666 Bright Red
3705 Dark Melon
743 Medium Yellow
3836 Light Grape
3840 Lavender Blue
799 Medium Delft Blue
798 Dark Delft Blue
016 Light Chartreuse

METHOD
Read the instructions for preparing the fabric and marking the centre on page 10. Following the chart and colour key, begin stitching at the centre over one square of Aida fabric using two strands of thread. Work backstitches using one strand of 3837, 740, 3845 and 703 thread for the matching balloon strings. Stitching area: 39 x 56 sts, 2¾ x 4in (7 x 10cm).

FINISHING
Press lightly from the wrong side on a padded surface. Mark from the centre 2½in (6.5cm) each side horizontally and 3½in (9cm) vertically (for a rectangle 5 x 7in [12.5 x 18cm]). Trim away the excess fabric and remove the centre basting threads. Apply double-sided tape to the inside of the card and centre the finished piece in the card window. Press to adhere to the tape. Hand-sew the fourth side closed.

BALLOON CARD

KEY

	NO STITCH
■	3837 DARK LAVENDER
■	740 TANGERINE
■	742 LIGHT TANGERINE
■	703 CHARTREUSE
■	3845 MEDIUM TURQUOISE
■	964 MEDIUM ORANGE
●	666 BRIGHT RED
■	3705 DARK MELON
■	743 MEDIUM YELLOW
■	3836 LIGHT GRAPE
■	3840 LAVENDER BLUE
■	799 MEDIUM DELFT BLUE
■	798 DARK DELFT BLUE
■	016 LIGHT CHARTREUSE

CIRCUS ELEPHANT

FABRIC 14-count white Aida fabric, one piece measuring 7 x 7in (18 x 18cm)
THREADS DMC six-strand embroidery thread, one skein of each colour listed
HOOP 3in (7.5cm)
STITCHING AREA 35 x 28 sts, 2½ x 2in (6.5 x 5cm)

Read the instructions for preparing the fabric and marking the centre on page 10. Following the chart and colour key, and using two strands of thread, start stitching at the centre over one square of Aida fabric. Work backstitches using two strands of 958 thread.

MAGICAL UNICORN

FABRIC 14-count white Aida fabric, one piece measuring 9 x 9in (23 x 23cm)
THREADS DMC six-strand embroidery thread, one skein of each colour listed
HOOP 5in (12.5cm)
STITCHING AREA 47 x 43 sts, 3½ x 3in (9 x 7.5cm)

Read the instructions for preparing the fabric and marking the centre on page 10. Following the chart and colour key, start stitching at the centre over one square of Aida fabric using two strands of thread. Work backstitches using one strand of 004 thread.

CIRCUS ELEPHANT

KEY

☐	NO STITCH
•	B5200 SNOW WHITE
■	958 DARK SEA GREEN
■	563 LIGHT JADE
■	033 FUCHSIA
■	703 CHARTREUSE
■	743 MEDIUM YELLOW
■	310 BLACK

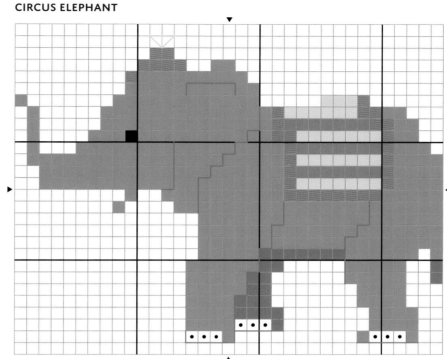

MAGICAL UNICORN

KEY

☐	NO STITCH
■	666 BRIGHT RED
■	970 LIGHT PUMPKIN
■	973 CANARY BRIGHT
■	703 CHARTREUSE
■	3843 ELECTRIC BLUE
■	3746 DARK BLUE VIOLET
■	3354 LIGHT DUSTY ROW
•	B5200 SNOW WHITE
■	004 DARK TIN

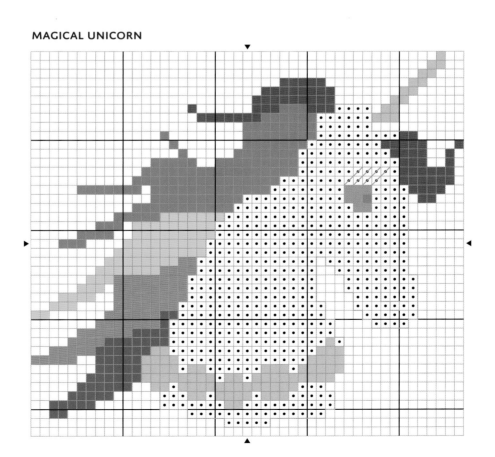

XYLOPHONE

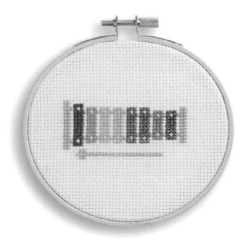

FABRIC 14-count white Aida fabric, one piece measuring 8 x 8in (20.5 x 20.5cm)
THREADS DMC six-strand embroidery thread, one skein of each colour listed
HOOP 4in (10cm)
STITCHING AREA 37 x 18 sts, 2½ x 1¼in (6.5 x 3cm)

Read the instructions for preparing the fabric and marking the centre on page 10. Following the chart and colour key, start stitching at the centre over one square of Aida fabric using two strands of thread.

STACKING TOY

FABRIC 14-count white Aida fabric, one piece measuring 8 x 8in (20.5 x 20.5cm)
THREADS DMC six-strand embroidery thread, one skein of each colour listed
HOOP 4in (10cm)
STITCHING AREA 27 x 35 sts, 2 x 2½in (5 x 6.5cm)

Read the instructions for preparing the fabric and marking the centre on page 10. Following the chart and colour key, start stitching at the centre over one square of Aida fabric using two strands of thread.

XYLOPHONE

KEY

	NO STITCH
	437 LIGHT TAN
	762 VERY LIGHT PEARL GREY
	973 CANARY BRIGHT
	817 VERY DARK CORAL RED
	970 LIGHT PUMPKIN
	958 DARK SEA GREEN
	016 LIGHT CHARTREUSE
	702 KELLY GREEN
	995 DARK ELECTRIC BLUE
	3837 ULTRA DARK LAVENDER

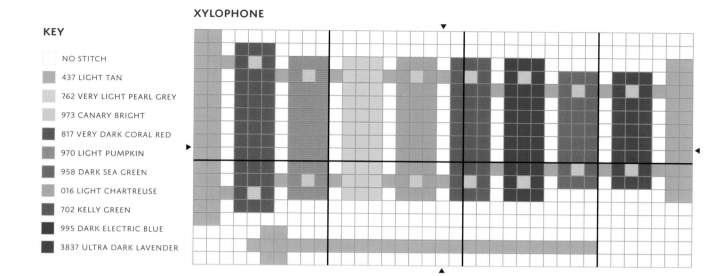

STACKING TOY

KEY

	NO STITCH
	606 BRIGHT ORANGE RED
	740 TANGERINE
	743 MEDIUM YELLOW
	703 CHARTREUSE
	3843 ELECTRIC BLUE
	3837 ULTRA DARK LAVENDER
	437 LIGHT TAN

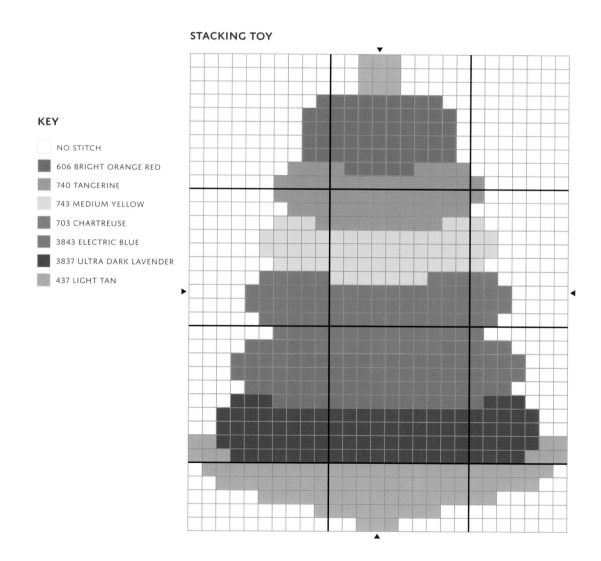

HELICOPTER

FABRIC 14-count white Aida fabric, one piece measuring 7 x 7in (18 x 18cm)
THREADS DMC six-strand embroidery thread, one skein of each colour listed
HOOP 3in (7.5cm)
STITCHING AREA 34 x 22 sts, 2½ x 1½in (6.5 x 4cm)

Read the instructions for preparing the fabric and marking the centre on page 10. Following the chart and colour key, start stitching at the centre over one square of Aida fabric using two strands of thread.

PAINTBOX

FABRIC 14-count white Aida fabric, one piece measuring 8 x 8in (20.5 x 20.5cm)
THREADS DMC six-strand embroidery thread, one skein of each colour listed
HOOP 4in (10cm)
STITCHING AREA 42 x 52 sts, 3 x 3¾in (7.5 x 9.5cm)

Read the instructions for preparing the fabric and marking the centre on page 10. Following the chart and colour key, start stitching at the centre over one square of Aida fabric using two strands of thread. Work backstitches using one strand of 004 thread.

HELICOPTER

KEY

- NO STITCH
- 958 DARK SEA GREEN
- 3840 LIGHT LAVENDER BLUE
- 742 LIGHT TANGERINE
- 970 LIGHT PUMPKIN
- 762 VERY LIGHT PEARL GREY

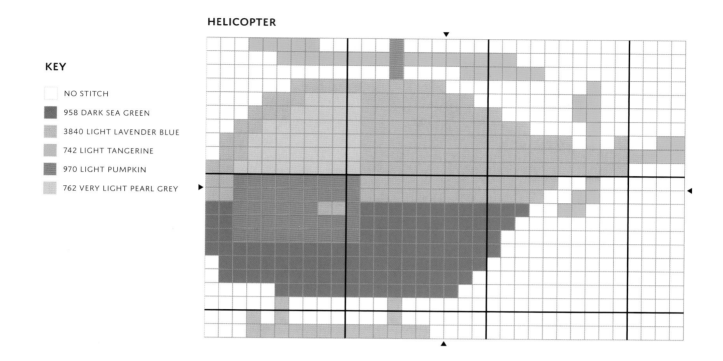

PAINTBOX

KEY

- NO STITCH
- 004 DARK TIN
- 666 BRIGHT RED
- 970 LIGHT PUMPKIN
- 973 BRIGHT CANARY
- 703 CHARTREUSE
- 3843 ELECTRIC BLUE
- 3746 DARK BLUE VIOLET
- 210 MEDIUM LAVENDER
- 3354 LIGHT DUSTY ROSE
- 003 MEDIUM TIN
- • 001 WHITE TIN
- 3831 DARK RASPBERRY
- 840 MEDIUM BEIGE BROWN

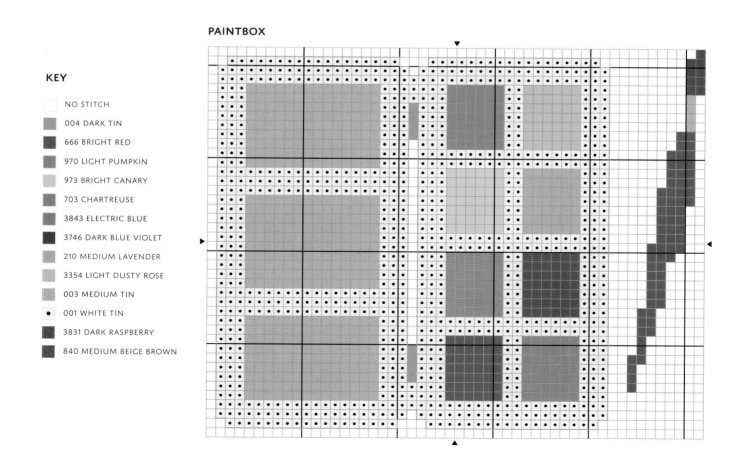

CIRCUS DRUM

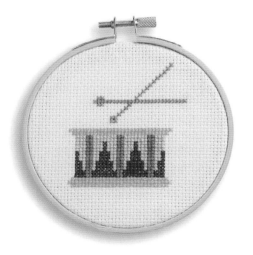

FABRIC 14-count white Aida fabric, one piece measuring 8 x 8in (20.5 x 20.5cm)
THREADS DMC six-strand embroidery thread, one skein of each colour listed
HOOP 4in (10cm)
STITCHING AREA 34 x 38 sts, 2½ x 2¾in (6.5 x 7cm)

Read the instructions for preparing the fabric and marking the centre on page 10. Following the chart and colour key, start stitching at the centre over one square of Aida fabric using two strands of thread.

TIN DRUM

FABRIC 14-count white Aida fabric, one piece measuring 7 x 7in (18 x 18cm)
THREADS DMC six-strand embroidery thread, one skein of each colour listed
HOOP 3in (7.5cm)
STITCHING AREA 26 x 31 sts, 2 x 2¼in (5 x 5.5cm)

Read the instructions for preparing the fabric and marking the centre on page 10. Following the chart and colour key, start stitching at the centre over one square of Aida fabric using two strands of thread. Work backstitches using one strand of 742 thread.

CIRCUS DRUM

KEY

- ☐ NO STITCH
- ■ 436 TAN
- ■ 817 VERY DARK CORAL RED
- ■ 3843 ELECTRIC BLUE
- ■ 3325 LIGHT BABY BLUE
- ■ 742 TANGERINE

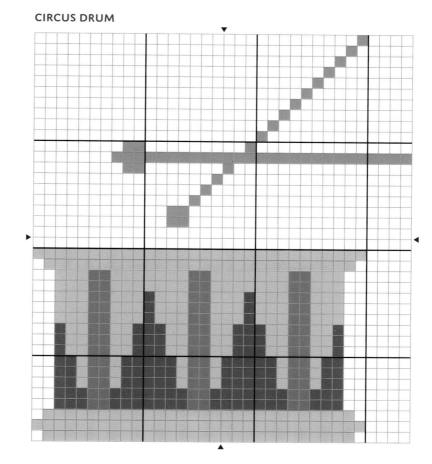

TIN DRUM

KEY

- ☐ NO STITCH
- ■ 742 LIGHT TANGERINE
- ■ 3842 DARK WEDGEWOOD
- ■ 958 DARK SEA GREEN
- • B5200 SNOW WHITE
- ■ 436 TAN

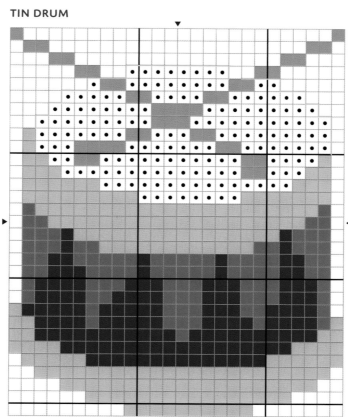

STEAM TRAIN

FABRIC 14-count white Aida fabric, one piece measuring 8 x 8in (20.5 x 20.5cm)
THREADS DMC six-strand embroidery thread, one skein of each colour listed
HOOP 4in (10cm)
STITCHING AREA 49 x 18 sts, 3½ x 1¼in (9 x 3cm)

Read the instructions for preparing the fabric and marking the centre on page 10. Following the chart and colour key, start stitching at the centre over one square of Aida fabric using two strands of thread.

SCHOOL BUS

FABRIC 14-count white Aida fabric, one piece measuring 9 x 9in (23 x 23cm)
THREADS DMC six-strand embroidery thread, one skein of each colour listed
HOOP 5in (12.5cm)
STITCHING AREA 50 x 22 sts, 3½ x 1½in (9 x 4cm)

Read the instructions for preparing the fabric and marking the centre on page 10. Following the chart and colour key, start stitching at the centre over one square of Aida fabric using two strands of thread. Work backstitches using one strand of 310 thread.

STEAM TRAIN

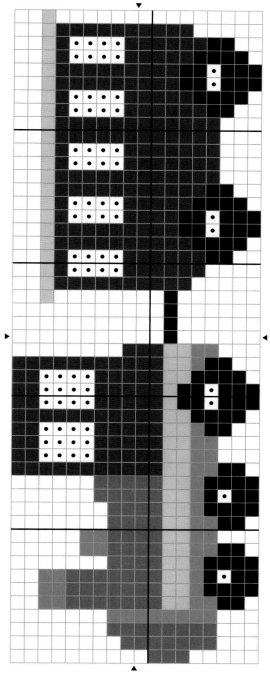

SCHOOL BUS

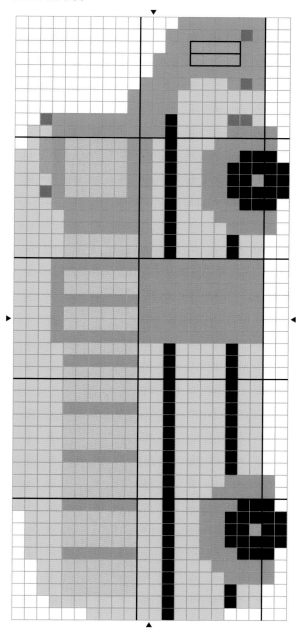

KEY

	NO STITCH
■	310 BLACK
■	817 VERY DARK CORAL RED
■	796 ROYAL BLUE
■	958 DARK SEA GREEN
■	742 LIGHT TANGERINE
•	B5200 SNOW WHITE

KEY

	NO STITCH
■	783 MEDIUM TOPAZ
■	800 PALE DELFT BLUE
■	606 BRIGHT ORANGE RED
■	648 BEAVER GREY
■	725 MEDIUM LIGHT TOPAZ
■	310 BLACK
■	436 TAN

RAINBOW CAT

FABRIC 14-count white Aida fabric, one piece measuring 9 x 9in (23 x 23cm)
THREADS DMC six-strand embroidery thread, one skein of each colour listed
HOOP 5in (12.5cm)
STITCHING AREA 48 x 48 sts, 3½ x 3½in (9 x 9cm)

Read the instructions for preparing the fabric and marking the centre on page 10. Following the chart and colour key, start stitching at the centre over one square of Aida fabric using two strands of thread. For the cat's whiskers, straight stitch using one strand of B5200 thread.

RAINBOW

FABRIC 14-count white Aida fabric, one piece measuring 9 x 9in (23 x 23cm)
THREADS DMC six-strand embroidery thread, one skein of each colour listed
HOOP 5in (12.5cm)
STITCHING AREA 53 x 41 sts, 3¾ x 2¾in (9.5 x 7.5cm)

Read the instructions for preparing the fabric and marking the centre on page 10. Following the chart and colour key, start stitching at the centre over one square of Aida fabric using two strands of thread.

RAINBOW CAT

KEY

	NO STITCH
■	666 BRIGHT RED
■	970 LIGHT PUMPKIN
■	973 BRIGHT CANARY
■	703 CHARTREUSE
■	3843 ELECTRIC BLUE
■	3746 BLUE VIOLET
•	B5200 SNOW WHITE

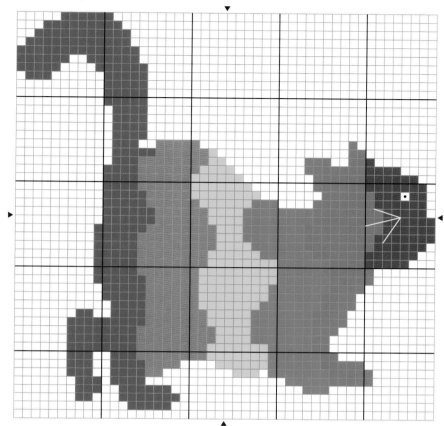

RAINBOW

KEY

	NO STITCH
■	827 VERY LIGHT BLUE
■	606 BRIGHT ORANGE RED
■	970 LIGHT PUMPKIN
■	973 BRIGHT CANARY
■	703 CHARTREUSE
■	995 ELECTRIC BLUE
■	3746 DARK BLUE VIOLET
■	3607 LIGHT PLUM

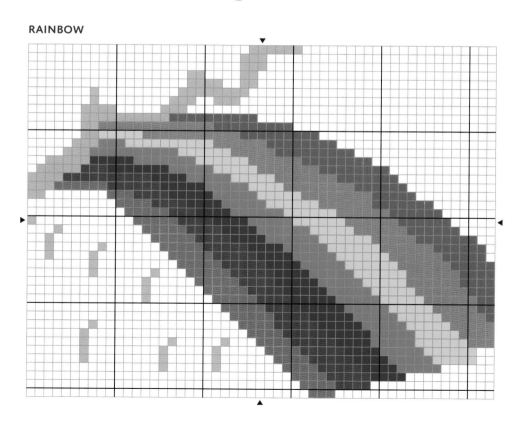

PINWHEEL

FABRIC 14-count white Aida fabric, one piece measuring 7 x 7in (18 x 18cm)
THREADS DMC six-strand embroidery thread, one skein of each colour listed
HOOP 3in (7.5cm)
STITCHING AREA 27 x 38 sts, 2 x 2¾in (5 x 7cm)

Read the instructions for preparing the fabric and marking the centre on page 10. Following the chart and colour key, start stitching at the centre over one square of Aida fabric using two strands of thread.

PUZZLE PIECES

FABRIC 14-count white Aida fabric, one piece measuring 8 x 8in (20.5 x 20.5cm)
THREADS DMC six-strand embroidery thread, one skein of each colour listed
HOOP 4in (10cm)
STITCHING AREA 35 x 35 sts, 2½ x 2½in (6.5 x 6.5cm)

Read the instructions for preparing the fabric and marking the centre on page 10. Following the chart and colour key, start stitching at the centre over one square of Aida fabric using two strands of thread.

PINWHEEL

KEY

☐ NO STITCH
■ 3746 BLUE VIOLET
■ 973 CANARY
■ 798 DARK DELFT BLUE
■ 958 DARK SEA GREEN
■ 703 CHARTREUSE
■ 433 MEDIUM BROWN
■ 349 DARK CORAL

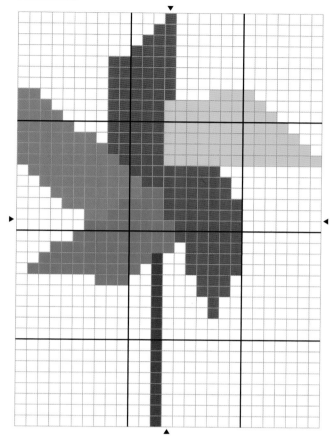

PUZZLE PIECES

KEY

☐ NO STITCH
■ 742 LIGHT TANGERINE
■ 702 KELLY GREEN
■ 995 ELECTRIC BLUE
■ 817 VERY DARK CORAL RED

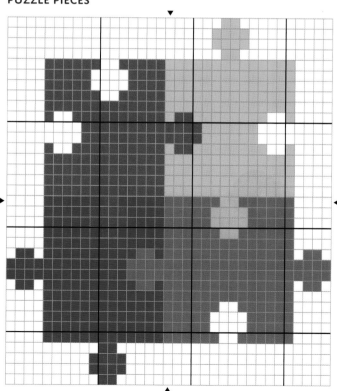

MERMAID

FABRIC 14-count pale blue Aida fabric, one piece measuring 8 x 8in (20.5 x 20.5cm)
THREADS DMC six-strand embroidery thread, one skein of each colour listed
HOOP 4in (10cm)
STITCHING AREA 36 x 42 sts, 2½ x 3in (6.5 x 7.5cm)

Read the instructions for preparing the fabric and marking the centre on page 10. Following the chart and colour key, start stitching at the centre over one square of Aida fabric using two strands of thread. Work backstitches using one strand of 943 thread.

BUILDING BRICKS

FABRIC 14-count white Aida fabric, one piece measuring 7 x 7in (18 x 18cm)
THREADS DMC six-strand embroidery thread, one skein of each colour listed
HOOP 3in (7.5cm)
STITCHING AREA 27 x 26 sts, 2 x 1¾in (5 x 4.5cm)

Read the instructions for preparing the fabric and marking the centre on page 10. Follow chart and colour key, stitching at the centre over one square of Aida fabric using two strands of thread.

MERMAID

KEY

☐	NO STITCH
•	B5200 SNOW WHITE
▨	019 MEDIUM LIGHT AUTUMN GOLD
▨	543 ULTRA VERY LIGHT BEIGE
▨	564 VERY LIGHT JADE
▨	959 MEDIUM SEA GREEN
▨	943 MEDIUM AQUAMARINE
▨	003 MEDIUM TIN

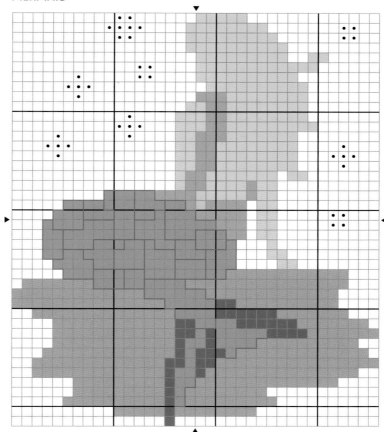

BUILDING BRICKS

KEY

☐	NO STITCH
▨	727 VERY LIGHT TOPAZ
▨	973 BRIGHT CANARY
▨	742 LIGHT TANGERINE
▨	349 DARK CORAL
▨	893 LIGHT CARNATION
▨	894 VERY LIGHT CARNATION
▨	796 DARK ROYAL BLUE
▨	798 DARK DELFT BLUE
▨	703 CHARTREUSE
▨	905 DARK PARROT GREEN

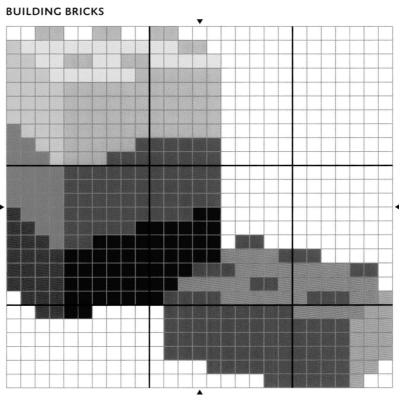

HOLLY SPRIG

SKILL LEVEL: EASY

*This mini sprig of holly will put everyone in the holiday spirit,
whether it's part of your annual decor or a special gift for a friend.*

YOU WILL NEED

MATERIALS
- 14-count pale blue Aida fabric, measuring one piece 5 x 6in (12.5 x 15cm)
- Basting thread
- One frame 3½ x 4½in (9 x 11.5cm)
- Tapestry needle, no. 24
- Scissors
- Double-sided tape

THREADS
DMC six-strand embroidery thread, one skein of each:
666 Bright Red
780 Topaz
704 Chartreuse
905 Dark Green

METHOD
Read the instructions for preparing the fabric and marking the centre on page 10. Following the chart and colour key, begin stitching at the centre over one square of Aida fabric using two strands of thread. Stitching area: 38 x 30 sts, 2¾ x 2¼in (7 x 5.5cm).

FINISHING
Press lightly from the wrong side on a padded surface. See framing instructions on page 15.

TIP
This motif would also make a very nice Christmas card when inserted into a purchased window card.

HOLLY SPRIG

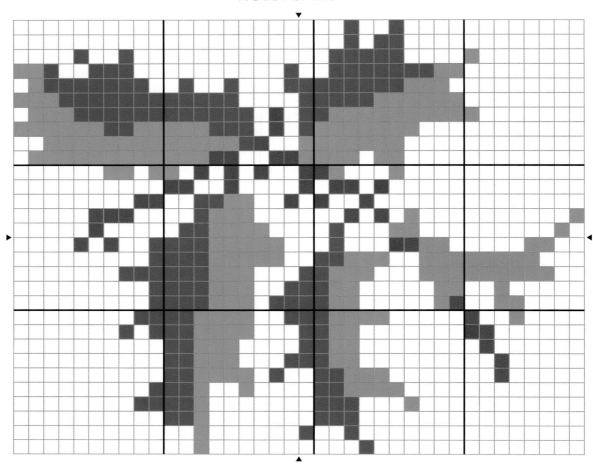

KEY

- ☐ NO STITCH
- ■ 666 RED
- ■ 780 TOPAZ
- ■ 704 CHARTREUSE
- ■ 905 DARK GREEN

SNOWFLAKE ORNAMENTS

SKILL LEVEL: INTERMEDIATE

The tiny beads around the edges of these ornaments make the season sparkle!

YOU WILL NEED

MATERIALS
For each ornament
- 14-count white Aida fabric, two pieces measuring 5 x 5in (13 x 13cm)
- Approx. 8in (20.5cm) of white satin ribbon
- Approx. 45 pearl glass seed beads
- Basting thread
- Tapestry needle, no. 24
- Small amount of fibrefill for stuffing
- Scissors

THREADS
DMC six-strand embroidery thread, one skein of each:
827 Light Blue
For finishing:
DMC pearl cotton 8 White

METHOD
Read the instructions for preparing the fabric and marking the centre on page 10. Following the chart and colour key, begin stitching at the centre over one square of Aida fabric using two strands of thread.

Stitching area Snowflake: 27 x 27 sts, 2 x 2in (5 x 5cm)
Stitching area Star: 25 x 25 sts, 1¾ x 1¾in (4.5 x 4.5cm)
Stitching area Crystal: 25 x 25 sts, 1¾ x 1¾in (4.5 x 4.5cm)

TIP
Before beginning to cross stitch an asymmetric design, mark the top of the fabric to avoid turning and stitching in the wrong direction.

FINISHING

Press lightly from the wrong side on a padded surface. Count three fabric squares away from the design on all four sides. Using pearl cotton, work a backstitch in each square around all four sides. Backstitch the same dimensions on an unstitched Aida backing fabric. Trim excess fabric away to three squares away from the backstitch lines. Fold fabric along the backstitch lines on both pieces. Press. With the wrong sides together, line up the backstitch. Attach the pearl cotton on the wrong side of one piece. Slip the needle through the tops of both backstitches, threading a bead at the same time. Pull tightly so the bead lies flat. Repeat for every stitch around three sides. Stuff with fibrefill, then sew the fourth side closed in the same manner to four stitches from the end. Fold the ribbon in half and insert into opening at the corner, then sew the remaining backstitches, making sure to catch the ribbon. Fasten securely.

KEY

☐ NO STITCH

▨ 827 LIGHT BLUE

STAR

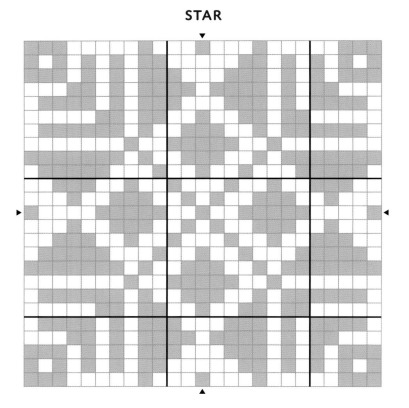

SNOWFLAKE

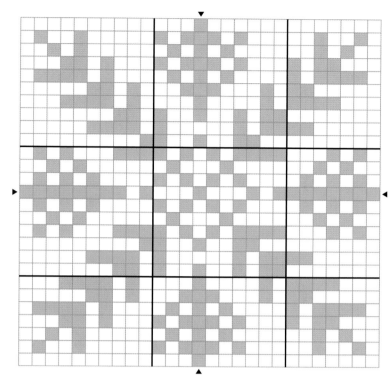

KEY

☐ NO STITCH

▨ 827 LIGHT BLUE

CRYSTAL

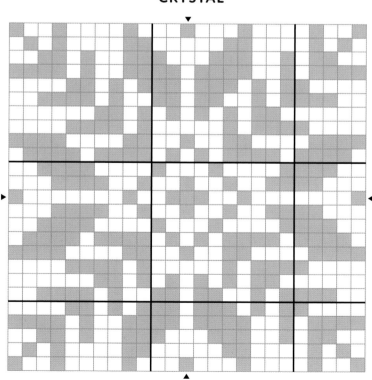

KEY

☐ NO STITCH

▨ 827 LIGHT BLUE

COOKIE GIFT TAGS

SKILL LEVEL: INTERMEDIATE

*Cross stitching on plastic canvas allows you to cut out shapes.
These holiday motifs can be used as gift tags, or they'd look equally
wonderful as ornaments hanging on the tree.*

YOU WILL NEED

MATERIALS
For each tag
- 14-count perforated plastic canvas, one piece measuring 5½ x 5½in (14 x 14cm)
- Tapestry needle, no. 24
- Small, sharp scissors
- 12in (30.5cm) decorative cord
- Two red buttons ¼in (6mm) for Gingerbread Cookie
- Self-adhesive white felt for backing

THREADS
DMC six-strand embroidery thread, one skein of each:

Gingerbread Cookie
310 Black
321 Red
906 Medium Green
407 Dark Desert Sand
700 Bright Green
B5200 Snow White

Heart Cookie
906 Medium Green
321 Red
3828 Brown

METHOD
Cross stitching on 14-count plastic canvas is very similar to cross stitching on Aida fabric. Each hole on the plastic canvas equals one hole on Aida cloth, so stitches are formed across a square of four holes. Plastic canvas does not bend, so you may have to use the stab method (taking the needle through and out the other side before making the second half of the stitch) of stitching. Begin a new thread with an away knot (page 11). Secure the thread by slipping the ending thread under the back of the previously worked stitches. Follow the chart as you would for working on fabric, using three strands of thread throughout.

Stitching area Gingerbread Cookie:
31 x 43 sts, 2¼ x 3in (5.5 x 7.5cm)
Stitching area Heart Cookie:
37 x 31 sts, 2½ x 2¼in (6.5 x 5.5cm)

FINISHING

After all the cross stitches are completed, sew on the buttons using the photo as a guide. Cut around the shape as follows: count the bars (not the holes) when cutting perforated plastic canvas. Always leave one bar on the outside of the stitches on all sides. Cut as close to the bars a possible, taking care not to cut any of the cross stitches. Place the cut-out shape on top of the self-adhesive felt and draw the outline on the felt. Cut out the felt shape and remove the adhesive paper. Fold the cord in half and place at the top to the adhesive side of the shape so that ½in (1.3cm) will be sandwiched between the two. Adhere the felt to the back of the cross stitch and cord. Press to secure.

GINGERBREAD COOKIE

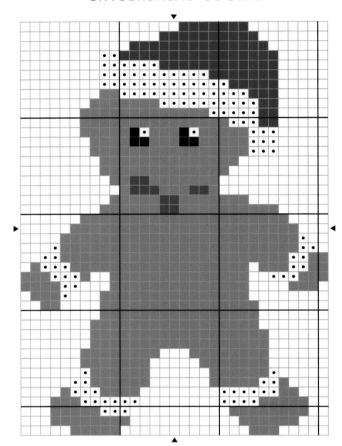

KEY

☐	NO STITCH
■	310 BLACK
■	321 RED
■	906 MEDIUM GREEN
■	407 DARK DESERT SAND
■	700 BRIGHT GREEN
•	B5200 SNOW WHITE

HEART COOKIE

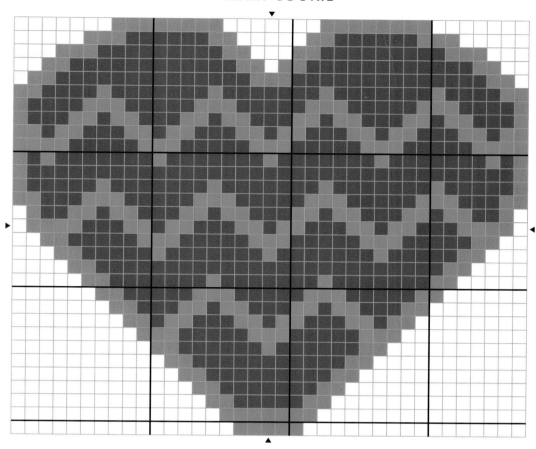

KEY

- NO STITCH
- 906 MEDIUM GREEN
- 321 RED
- 3828 BROWN

FESTIVE TOWEL

SKILL LEVEL: EASY

Greet your holiday guests with a special towel that celebrates the season.

YOU WILL NEED

MATERIALS
- Velour towel measuring 12 x 19.5in (30.5 x 49.5cm) with 14-count Aida inset
- Basting thread
- Tapestry needle, no. 24
- Scissors

THREADS
DMC six-strand embroidery thread, one skein:
321 Red

METHOD
Read the instructions for preparing the fabric and marking the centre on page 10. Following the chart and colour key, begin stitching at the centre over one square of Aida band using two strands of thread. Stitching area: 59 x 25 sts, 4¼ x 1¾in (10.5 x 7cm).

FINISHING
Remove the basting threads. Press lightly from the wrong side on a padded surface.

TIP
Try changing the snowflake colour to match your decor.

FESTIVE TOWEL

KEY

☐ NO STITCH

■ 321 RED

JEWELLED EGG

FABRIC 14-count white Aida fabric, one piece measuring 8 x 8in (20 x 20cm)
THREADS DMC six-strand embroidery thread, one skein of each colour listed
HOOP 4in (10cm)
STITCHING AREA 25 x 40 sts, 1¾ x 2¾in (4.5 x 7cm)

Read the instructions for preparing the fabric and marking the centre on page 10. Following the chart and colour key, start stitching at the centre over one square of Aida fabric using two strands of thread.

SPRING BASKET

FABRIC 14-count white Aida fabric, one piece measuring 8 x 8in (20 x 20cm)
THREADS DMC six-strand embroidery thread, one skein of each colour listed
HOOP 4in (10cm)
STITCHING AREA 39 x 43 sts, 2¾ x 3in (7 x 7.5cm)

Read the instructions for preparing the fabric and marking the centre on page 10. Following the chart and colour key, start stitching at the centre over one square of Aida fabric using two strands of thread. Work backstitches using one strand of 3772 and 517 thread.

JEWELLED EGG

KEY

KEY

☐ NO STITCH

■ 552 MEDIUM VIOLET

☐ 742 LIGHT TANGERINE

■ 3766 LIGHT PEACOCK BLUE

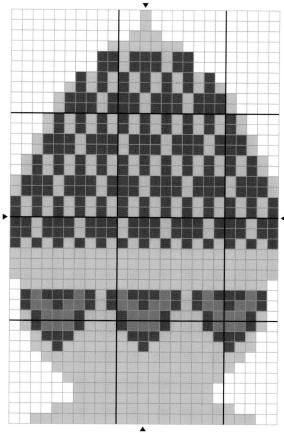

SPRING BASKET

KEY

☐ NO STITCH

■ 519 SKY BLUE

■ 517 DARK WEDGEWOOD

■ 3607 LIGHT PLUM

☐ 973 BRIGHT CANARY

■ 3772 VERY DARK DESERT SAND

■ 970 LIGHT PUMPKIN

■ 950 LIGHT DESERT SAND

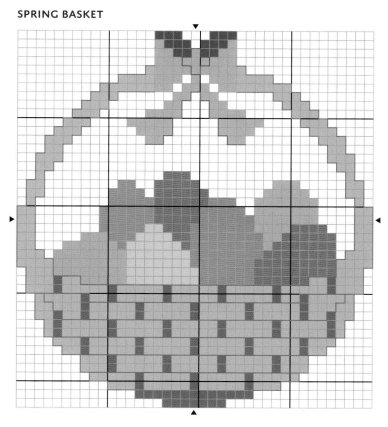

WITCH CAT

FABRIC 14-count white Aida fabric, one piece measuring 8 x 8in (20.5 x 20.5cm)
THREADS DMC six-strand embroidery thread, one skein of each colour listed
HOOP 4in (10cm)
STITCHING AREA 40 x 39 sts, 2¾ x 2¾in (7 x 7cm)

Read the instructions for preparing the fabric and marking the centre on page 10. Following the chart and colour key, start stitching at the centre over one square of Aida fabric using two strands of thread. Work backstitches using one strand of 900 thread.

HALLOWEEN PUMPKIN

FABRIC 14-count white Aida fabric, one piece measuring 8 x 8in (20.5 x 20.5cm)
THREADS DMC six-strand embroidery thread, one skein of each colour listed
HOOP 4in (10cm)
STITCHING AREA 41 x 38 sts, 3 x 2¾in (7.5 x 7cm)

Read the instructions for preparing the fabric and marking the centre on page 10. Following the chart and colour key, start stitching at the centre over one square of Aida fabric using two strands of thread. Work backstitches using one strand of 900 and 987 thread.

WITCH CAT

KEY

	NO STITCH
	783 MEDIUM TOPAZ
	900 DARK BURNT ORANGE
	310 BLACK
	906 MEDIUM PARROT GREEN
	970 LIGHT PUMPKIN

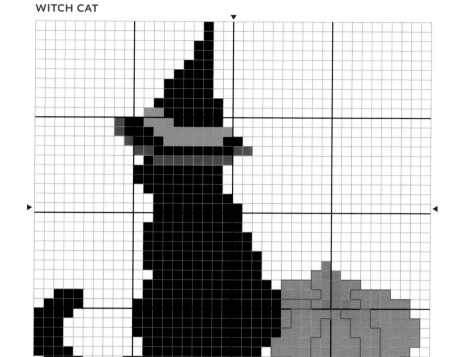

HALLOWEEN PUMPKIN

KEY

	NO STITCH
	310 BLACK
	900 DARK BURNT ORANGE
	987 DARK FOREST GREEN
	906 MEDIUM PARROT GREEN
	740 TANGERINE

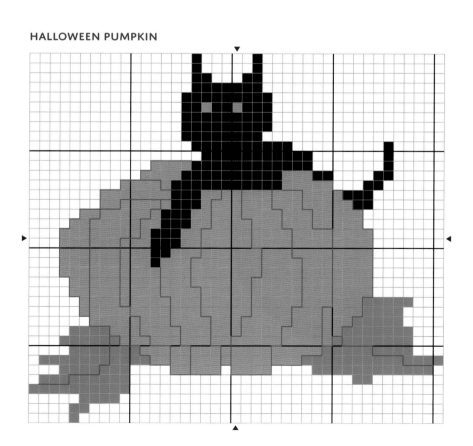

FLOATING GHOSTS

FABRIC 14-count navy blue Aida fabric, one piece measuring 8 x 8in (20.5 x 20.5cm)
THREADS DMC six-strand embroidery thread, one skein of each colour listed
HOOP 4in (10cm)
STITCHING AREA 32 x 35 sts, 2¼ x 2½in (5.5 x 6.5cm)

Read the instructions for preparing the fabric and marking the centre on page 10. Following the chart and colour key, start stitching at the centre over one square of Aida fabric using two strands of thread.

MENORAH

FABRIC 14-count white Aida fabric, one piece measuring 9 x 9in (23 x 23cm)
THREADS DMC six-strand embroidery thread, one skein of each colour listed
HOOP 5in (12.5cm)
STITCHING AREA 42 x 47 sts, 3 x 3¼in (7.5 x 8cm)

Read the instructions for preparing the fabric and marking the centre on page 10. Following the chart and colour key, start stitching at the centre over one square of Aida fabric using two strands of thread.

FLOATING GHOSTS

KEY

NO STITCH

• B5200 SNOW WHITE

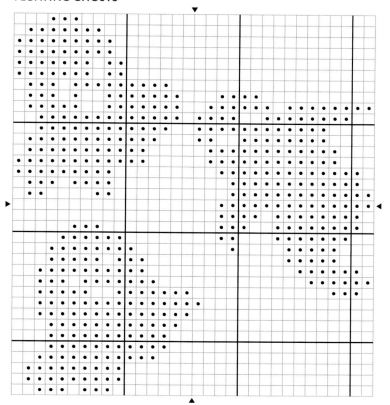

MENORAH

KEY

NO STITCH

798 DARK DEFLT BLUE

666 BRIGHT RED

743 MEDIUM YELLOW

800 PALE DELFT BLUE

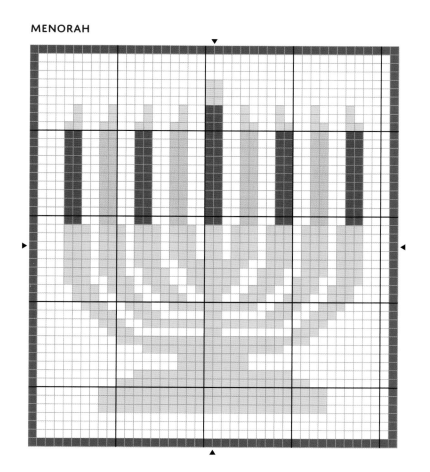

STAR OF DAVID

FABRIC 14-count white Aida fabric, one piece measuring 7 x 7in (18 x 18cm)
THREADS DMC six-strand embroidery thread, one skein of each colour listed
HOOP 3in (7.5cm)
STITCHING AREA 37 x 34 sts, 2¾ x 2½in (7 x 6.5cm)

Read the instructions for preparing the fabric and marking the centre on page 10. Following the chart and colour key, start stitching at the centre over one square of Aida fabric using two strands of thread.

ICY PENGUIN

FABRIC 14-count white Aida fabric, one piece measuring 8 x 8in (20.5 x 20.5cm)
THREADS DMC six-strand embroidery thread, one skein of each colour listed
HOOP 4in (10cm)
STITCHING AREA 30 x 39 sts, 2 x 3¼in (5 x 8cm)

Read the instructions for preparing the fabric and marking the centre on page 10. Following the chart and colour key, start stitching at the centre over one square of Aida fabric using two strands of thread. Work backstitches using one strand of 310 thread.

STAR OF DAVID

KEY

- NO STITCH
- 743 MEDIUM YELLOW
- 798 DARK DELFT BLUE
- 800 PALE DELFT BLUE

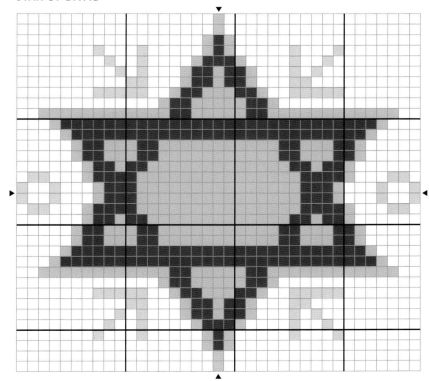

ICY PENGUIN

KEY

- NO STITCH
- 310 BLACK
- 666 BRIGHT RED
- • B5200 SNOW WHITE
- 827 VERY LIGHT BLUE
- 415 PEARL GREY
- 725 TOPAZ

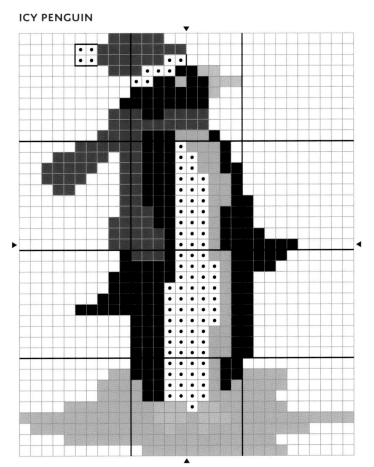

HOLIDAY PENGUIN

FABRIC 14-count white Aida fabric, one piece measuring 9 x 9in (23 x 23cm)
THREADS DMC six-strand embroidery thread, one skein of each colour listed
HOOP 5in (12.5cm)
STITCHING AREA 45 x 47 sts, 3¼ x 3¼in (8 x 8cm)

Read the instructions for preparing the fabric and marking the centre on page 10. Following the chart and colour key, start stitching at the centre over one square of Aida fabric using two strands of thread. Work backstitches using one strand of 310 thread.

SKATING SANTA

FABRIC 14-count white Aida fabric, one piece measuring 10 x 10in (25.5 x 25.5cm)
THREADS DMC six-strand embroidery thread, one skein of each colour listed
HOOP 6in (15.5cm)
STITCHING AREA 56 x 58 sts, 4 x 4¼in (10 x 10.5cm)

Read the instructions for preparing the fabric and marking the centre on page 10. Following the chart and colour key, start stitching at the centre over one square of Aida fabric using two strands of thread. Work backstitches using one strand of 310 and 414 thread. French knot using two strands of 334 thread, wrapping twice for the eye.

HOLIDAY PENGUIN

KEY

- NO STITCH
- 666 BRIGHT RED
- 725 TOPAZ
- 905 DARK PARROT GREEN
- 310 BLACK
- • B5200 SNOW WHITE
- 780 ULTRA VERY DARK TOPAZ

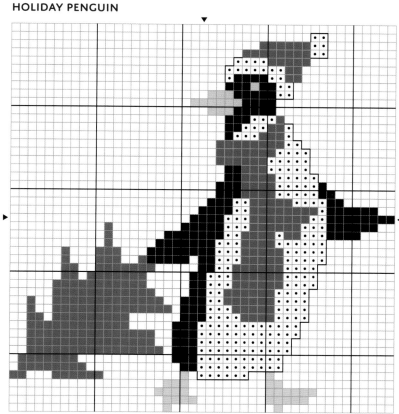

SKATING SANTA

KEY

- NO STITCH
- 334 MEDIUM BABY BLUE
- 414 PEARL GREY
- 666 BRIGHT RED
- 905 DARK PARROT GREEN
- 310 BLACK
- 605 VERY LIGHT CRANBERRY
- • B5200 SNOW WHITE
- 827 VERY LIGHT BLUE

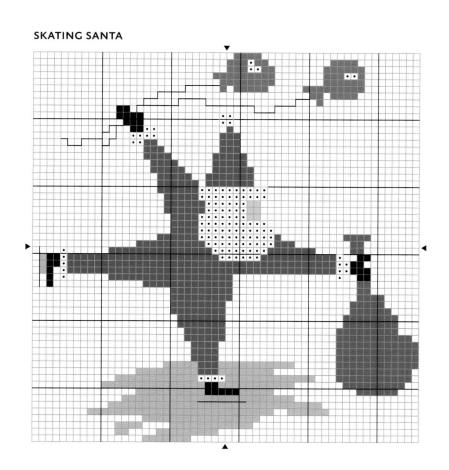

RESOURCES

Fabric, felt, thread and embroidery hoops:
Amazon – amazon.co.uk
Hobbycraft – hobbycraft.co.uk

Frames, greetings cards and cushion pads:
Amazon – amazon.co.uk
Dunelm – dunelm.com
Michaels – michaels.com

Embroidery floss and pearl cotton:
Anchor – anchorcrafts.com
DMC – dmc.com

ACKNOWLEDGEMENTS

I would like to thank the talented staff at Quail Publishing for creating such a beautiful book. Special thanks to my friend, Trisha Malcolm, for encouraging me to pick up my embroidery needle again, and thanks to my editor, Susan Elliott. I could not have created the embroideries without the support of my family and friends who spurred me on during the good days and through these challenging times. Lastly, I owe all this to a wonderful lady, Joan Toggitt, who guided me on my long and wonderful career in the embroidery world, even long after she had left us. She was, and still is, my guardian angel.

INDEX

To order a book, contact:

GMC Publications Ltd

Castle Place, 166 High Street,

Lewes, East Sussex,

BN7 1XU

United Kingdom

Tel: +44 (0)1273 488005

www.gmcbooks.com